Effective Copywriting Strategy for Money & Sales

Learn the secret formula copywriters use for Online Digital Marketing, Web Content Creation, Business Email, & SEO.

By David Marcel

Copyright

guaranteed or warranted to produce any particular results, and the advice and strategies contained herein are not suitable for every individual. By providing information or links to other companies or websites, the publisher and the author do not guarantee, approve or endorse the information or products available at any linked websites or mentioned companies, or persons, nor does a link indicate any association with or endorsement by the publisher or author. It is offered or sold with the understanding that neither the publisher nor the author is engaged in rendering legal, accounting or other professional service. If legal advice or other expert assistance is required, the services of a competent professional should be sought. Neither the publisher nor the author shall be liable for any loss or loss of profit or any other commercial damages, including but not limited to special, incidental, consequential, or other damages.

Table of Contents

Ch. 1: Introduction

In this emerging information age, everybody is a writer—whether you want to be one or not. That is to say, if you've ever written a blog, testimonial, forum post, webpage, email, or social media post (like on Facebook, Instagram, Pinterest, or LinkedIn), then you've probably written *something* about a product or service. Perhaps it was text about a product you sell. Or perhaps it was a recommendation you made to a friend.

In either case, did you notice that the words you wrote, were able to influence the buying behavior of the person who read your words?

Take a moment to appreciate what a powerful concept this is. You typed something on a keyboard in one city, and your acquaintance (perhaps living hundreds of miles away), read your text, and decided to *part with their hard-earned cash*, and buy the product you recommended. There's a name for people who do this sort of activity.

A person who writes persuasive text—designed to coax a consumer into purchasing a product, is called a "copywriter."

So, whether you know it or not, you're probably *already* a copywriter.

Moreover, if you've ever signed up to a website, downloaded an eBook, or bought a gadget online, then you've been subject to the enchanting words, of one copywriter or another.

Indeed, no matter where you look (in the real world or online), you see words. (Lots and lots of words.) And each word, of each sentence you read, was carefully selected by a copywriter—whose sole intent was to grab your attention, and convince you that *his product* is worthy of your money.

As you stroll around your local mall, or browse through cyberspace, I hope the importance of this skillset (copywriting) is crystal clear to you. Though the history of copywriting goes back centuries, the *skill* is more *in-demand* now, than ever before. Why? Because there are more literate people on earth now, than ever before.

Just a few decades ago, copywriting was mostly about creating captivating content for print publications—like newspapers and magazines. But the internet has brought forth a cornucopia of advertisement media, and new international consumers—all waiting to devour it.

While the medium may have changed, the rules are still the same. Because, the rules of copywriting are timeless.

So, if you work in any sort of industry, that uses the written word, then it's in your interest to develop this skillset.

Now, getting customers to see the value in any given product, can be difficult. People are busy. And writing words that get attention is not an easy undertaking. But, new writers need not be intimidated by the process. Because, even if you've never published a single word before, you can still be a *great copywriter*. Because great copywriting is not about creating art, or poetry, or analyzing a Shakespearean sonnet. Rather, it's about "speaking the customer's language," and knowing which words to use, and which *triggers* make him want to buy your product.

A copywriter need not be a master wordsmith. In fact, weaving colorful sentences together (with flowery prose) is often a detriment in copywriting. Because the sales letters that use a limited lexicon (with drop-dead simple language), tend to make the most money anyway.

The trick to writing copy that sells, is to apply the formulas—that professional copywriters have been developing for centuries. Until quite recently, you'd only know these tricks, if you worked in an advertising agency, or spent long hours—testing various marketing ploys. But, in this book, we've attempted to surmise the most important aspects of this enterprise, and break down these techniques into easily digestible exercises. When you learn to spot the *innate buying triggers* (of the human subconscious), then the chore of copywriting will actually become easy, and fun!

Are you ready to begin?

Then grab some coffee. And let's explore the wonderful (weird) world of copywriting.

Ch. 2: What is Copywriting?

We'll start off this book by defining our terms. This task is actually a little trickier than you might think. Because in the vast field of content-creation, one term will often step on the toes of another term. And even industry executives sometimes use the terms incorrectly!

This is partly due to the fact that the terms in question, look and sound quite similar.

"Copy, Copywriter, Copyeditor, Content Writer, and Copyright."

See what I mean?

Let's define each of these terms now.

What is a "Copywriter?"

A copywriter is a person who writes text for advertisements, or other marketing material. His aim is to compose a persuasive message—that prompts a target consumer to perform an action. This action might entail: buying a product, downloading an eBook, signing up to a website, sharing a link, making a phone call, etc, etc... Thus:

Copywriting is the art and science of turning words into sales.

It's about getting the attention of a specific audience, and motivating them to do something. It's about producing a creative, effective, and evocative message—specifically designed to persuade and sell. Thus, it is an essential tool for any business—looking to spread the word about their product or service.

What is "Copy?"

The term "copy" refers to the textual elements in a piece of marketing material.

- For example, when you're referring to the "copy" in a magazine, you're typically referring to the words that cover the adverts on its glossy pages.
- If you're an online marketer, and you're referring to the "copy" on a website, then you're usually talking about the HTML text—that holds (and formats) the words on each webpage.

The term "copy" is usually synonymous with the term "words." Copywriters are the people who produce these words. Or, to put it another way:

"Copywriters produce copy."

That's their job.

What is a "Copyeditor?"

A copyeditor is a person who reviews text before publication. Often, a copyeditor is paid to look for grammar or spelling mistakes. But they may also be asked to search for technical (industry-specific) errors in a document too.

Though the words sound similar, a copyeditor is usually *not* a copywriter. Remember, a copywriter's job is to write words that persuade you to buy something. But the copyeditor's job is to find errors in a document.

The terms copyeditor, copyreader, and proofreader are all quite comparable, and they're often used synonymously.

What is "Copyright?"

The word "copyright" (with an "r") sounds like the word "copywriter" (with a "w"). But actually the words are not related.

The word "copyright" refers to the ***legal*** right to print, sell, or reproduce a literary (or artistic) work. For example, if you hold the *copyright* to the novel "Harry Potter and the Philosopher's Stone", that means you have the right to print and sell this book. (And you'd be rich indeed.)

What is a "Content Writer"?

A Content Writer (or "Content Creator") is a person that creates or produces content. This might be in the form of a blog post, YouTube video, webpage, instruction manual, email newsletter, etc.

A content creator is often a skilled writer. But they might also specialize in other creative tasks, like background research, photography, Search Engine Optimization (SEO), or even video editing.

Some "content writers" are also "copywriters." But most are not.

So, let's review one last time. A "copywriter" is a person who produces words that try to *sell you something*. Ideally, he "turns words into cash"—which is what we're most concerned with in this book.

Ch. 3: Getting Started with Copywriting

So now that we've got our terms straight, let's start learning how to write good "copy" (i.e. how to be a good copywriter).

The art and science of Copywriting has been practiced for centuries. But with the advent of the Information Age, the skillset is in more demand now, than ever before. If you've ever signed up to a website, downloaded an eBook, or bought cat food online, then you've been subject to the enchantment of a copywriter.

There are good and bad copywriters in this world, just as there are with every other skill. So let's talk about how to be a good one.

What is Good Copywriting?

There's a big difference between so-so and well-crafted copy. Effective copywriting does not require you to beat a person over the head with your message. Nor does it entail creating a gaudy textual display of misplaced capitalization and bold typefaces. Rather, good copywriting is about composing a persuasive message—that stands on its own merit—without an overabundance of "salesy" language.

Remember, copywriting is an **art and a science**. So, as with any type of human writing, it's impossible to quantify exactly *why* one paragraph is "good" while another is "bad." There is a subjective element as well, of course. But, below, we've listed some rules to get you started producing excellent copy.

Rule 1: Good copywriting is for a specific audience.

Ultimately, a properly targeted ad will fall upon the eyes of a specific audience. Hence, your goal is to write and promote your content, in such a way as to ensure that your target market will respond to it.

Because of this, market research is often the first step in copywriting. Work hard to evaluate your customers, and maintain a demographic profile for your target consumer. Our primary goal in marketing is to advertise in places where we can find new customers, who are similar to our current *paying* customers.

Rule 2: Good writing addresses the customers as "you," not "we."

Be careful with the language you use when communicating with your audience. Don't sound "overtly professional" in your marketing material. And avoid the "third person." Instead, write in a "conversational tone," in the first or second person. Writing in this style often aids in connecting the main points in your copy, to relatable events in your reader's lives. The word "we" is typically *bad form* in the world of copywriting. Why? Because your readers are interested in hearing from "you," not "we." Additionally, they are just as curious to hear about themselves, using the word "you."

So, talk about **their** problems, their needs, their desires, their memories, and their future, etc. All the copy you write should be *about* your target prospect. Not some generalized "we."

However, there is one copywriting trope which often breaks this rule. And that is when you're providing some sort of corporate pledge to your reader. For example:

"Your food will be delivered in 30-minutes or less."

It's acceptable to use "we" in sentences such as this—which reveal some sort of "promise," or "brand commitment" to your audience.

Rule 3: Good copywriting promises a unique benefit to the audience.

Your audience has many options to consider. So what is it (exactly) that makes your marketing efforts different?

Why should people choose your product?

What makes *you* different?

Novelty is important in product sales. So, be sure to focus on some unique element of your product—that makes it distinguishable from the plethora of other products out there.

Be familiar with your product's USP (Unique Selling Proposition). A "USP" is a pledge (about your product) that you make to your potential customer—in which you exclaim the virtues of a novel benefit that your product provides.

Ideally, this product attribute should be one that your competition currently does not offer.

Here are a few examples from some famous companies:

- **FedEx**: "When it absolutely, positively has to be there overnight."
- **Domino's Pizza**: "You get fresh, hot pizza delivered to your door in 30 minutes or less—or it's free."
- **M&M's**: "Melts in your mouth, not in your hand."

Rule 4: Good copywriting is not information-heavy.

Nothing scares off people more than a wall of text. Our lives are busy, and we simply don't have time to comb through every marketing presentation—hunting for the absolute best deal.

So, if your ad copy is too long, you'll risk losing the attention of your audience. Instead, strive for brevity. Tell your audience what they need to know, and keep it simple.

Rule 5: Good copywriting contains proof that the product works.

Humans are scared and anxious creatures. Unsure of themselves. And unsure about others. One of our most important jobs (as copywriters), is to curtail this anxiety. And one of the best ways to do this is to offer proof (in one form or another), that our product works.

This proof typically comes in the form of a customer testimonial, an award from an industry leader, a story in a major newspaper, a before and after photo, etc.

In any case, work hard to gather evidence of your product's effectiveness. For this is often the most persuasive marketing element in your copy.

Rule 6: Move the customer towards your Call-to-Action.

Remember, most people need a shove in the right direction. Your marketing copy should guide people toward your Call-to-Action. And, when they get there, their next course of action should be blatantly obvious.

- Are they supposed to click a link?
- Are they supposed to call this phone number?
- Are they supposed to "Add to Cart"?

Whatever your Call-to-Action is, make it conspicuous.

Rule 7: Track and Test.

These days, and especially when it comes to marketing in the digital space, you must maintain tracking statistics—for all your marketing efforts. This is the only way to really know what is working, and what is not. Fortunately, there are thousands of different stats tracking tools to choose from. And each industry may use slightly different metrics to reveal sales data. But pivotal to our discussion here, is that you get in the habit of using some sort of objective measure, to determine if your marketing efforts are working, or not.

How do you know if you're a "good copywriter"?

Applying the above rules will not necessarily make your copy good. When it comes to human creative efforts (like novels, film scripts, or poetry) then how "good" a piece is, might be dictated by the whims of a small coterie of literary critics.

However, when it comes to copywriting, there are no such pretensions. Remember, in copywriting, our only goal is to "turn our words into cash." Hence, in copywriting, we're afforded the luxury of having an *objective measure* by which to gauge the success (or failure) of any given piece of copy.

"Good copywriting" is that which succeeds in converting customers into buyers.

Note that this is a niche-specific enterprise. The copy you'd use to sell diamonds to aristocrats, is not the same, as the copy you'd use to sell flashlights to backpackers. And some markets are simply bigger (and more moneyed) than others. But, ultimately, you know you've written *good copy*, when it incites your target clientele to hand over their hard-earned cash, for your product or service.

The 3 Parts of the Copywriter's Message

In general, you can break the copywriter's product, down into just three parts:

1. The Headline
2. The Copy
3. The Call-to-Action

The Headline is that bold blurb of text that lies along the top of a document, and tries to grab the reader's attention.

The Copy, refers to all the words below the headline—that make up the majority of your advertising message.

The Call-to-Action is the final advertising element, which prompts the user to perform an action. In traditional copywriting the Call-to-Action might request that the reader "call this phone number" or "inquire today!" On web documents, however, this Call-to-Action is often paired with an "Add to Cart" button—that moves the reader on to a credit card processing webpage or PayPal checkout screen.

A good copywriter will craft each of these three elements, to work harmoniously toward his ultimate goal—of getting you to buy something.

We'll discuss each of these three components in the following chapters.

Ch. 4: The Headline

Go to your favorite news website, and glance at the ads displayed along the side. Blur your eyes a bit, so that the text is fuzzy, and merely skirts across your field of vision. That about sums up how people really see your advertisement copy. Most people don't spend much time reading ad copy, of course. They don't pay much attention to newspaper or magazine ads, Facebook ads, Television ads, or any other ads in their life.

- So, why should your ad be any different?
- What can *you* do—to grab the reader's attention?

That's where the (ever-so-important) "headline" comes in. The main job of the headline is to attract readers—so that they'll pause and glance at the advertisement copy too.

Note the emotions you feel when you're standing in line at the grocery store checkout counter. Note the flurry of sensationalized tabloid headlines that buzz around you. How are these headlines affecting you? These headlines were crafted in such a way that they beckon for your attention immediately. They try to instill a sense of fascination, and create anticipation.

Let's learn how they do that.

The famous copywriter Joseph Sugarman, described a headline as "a slippery slope"—in which the reader would first, be "sucked in" to reading the headline, and then the subheading, and then the first line of the copy, and then the second line, and so forth. Ideally, we want to create this "slope of interest," for the reader to fall down.

Traditionally, we start with a nice, big headline at the top of the ad—to capture the viewer's attention. Then, a relevant, appealing image is placed under the headline. And then, the ad copy is written—that compliments both the image and the headline, and fills up the rest of the available ad space.

The headline is the most crucial part of this process. The famous website CopyBlogger.com has estimated that, out of the ten people who see your ad, eight will read the headline. And, only two will proceed to read the rest of your copy. So if you want more people to stay on board, your headline needs to be as good as possible.

5 Principles for Creating Great Headlines

Every copywriter has their own style of course. And, as you progress in your own copywriting career, you should work to develop your own style as well. But, to start you off, we've listed five foundation guidelines, to help you write unique headlines today.

Principle 1. Use a Relevant Headline

Just getting visitors to come to your advertisement is not enough. Many young marketers might try tricks, to get people to click on a button or perform an action—such as writing "Do not click this button," on the ad headline. But this is a gimmick.

Even if your little trick succeeds in getting 90 percent of your traffic to click through, the audience will not take further action after they arrive at your page, like purchase your product. The reason is that the wording of your ad doesn't relate to the desires of your target audience—who actually might potentially need your product.

Therefore, our goal in copywriting is not to lure every eyeball. Rather, we want to drive the traffic that actually converts. That's why we must use a relevant headline.

Principle 2. Speak to a Target Audience

Part of our job (as copywriters) is to filter out the uninterested readers. This is done by creating a headline that speaks to a targeted group of people who will be attracted to your product or service.

So don't be afraid to add a large helping of "specificity" to your headline copy.

Principle 3. Use Numbers

One of the oldest (and most effective) tricks to catch attention, is to use numbers in your headline. For reasons unknown, people are attracted to numerical values in ad copy. Here are some examples:

- The top 5 ways to earn passive income online!

Thomas Pearson

- 10 easiest ketogenic foods to cook this Summer.
- 20 ways to make money from Instagram!

You can even use numbers twice in your headlines. For example:

- Top 5 ways to earn passive income—up to $1,000 per month.
- 15 ketogenic foods to cook this Christmas—in only 15 minutes.
- The 25 quickest ways to earn money from Instagram in 15 minutes per day.

Number arrangements like this can be extremely effective. And note that people seem to respond best to odd numbers like "97", not even numbers like "98."

Principle 4. Add favorable Adjectives

After reading the initial headline, customers always ask themselves:

"Why should I read more?"

To answer this question for your reader, your headline should use adjectives that describe the benefit of continuing to read your copy. So, use beneficial adjectives like:

- *Easiest*
- *Quickest*

23

- *Useful*
- *Effective*
- *and Affordable*

Principle 5. Ask a Question

This hack often works best for the subheading. A proper subheading adds interest and value to the headline and your copy. It makes the headline better.

Most people scan the copy to find out if it provides the information they are looking for, or if it can solve their problem. Therefore, write your subheading in the form of a question so that the readers can see what answers they will get from the copy.

The "4-U Formula" for Headline Creation

Now we'll introduce you to a popular headline technique called "The 4-U Formula." It can work wonders for your headline, and improve the odds that your audience will actually read your copy.

This formula contains four elements—each starting with the letter "U." When composing your headline, try to make it:

1. **Useful**. Think about the content you read on a typical day—while scrolling through Facebook or checking your mail. Which bit of content did you prefer, or which one piqued your interest? To find your audience, understand what is most helpful to them. In this way,

you will know where they are, and you can identify their problems and offer solutions.

2. **Unique**. Uniqueness is critical because if the audience already knows the information or benefits you are offering, they won't bother to read your copy. Think about it. When you're searching Google and 10 similar links popup, we tend to click on the most unique one. Why? The answer is that unusual headlines make the copy stick out more. So, if you can do anything to add novelty to your headline, consider trying it.

3. **Ultra-specific**. It is possible for your headline to be useful, and unique, without being specific enough. However, the more specific your headline is, the more valuable it will be. Highly specific headlines often work because the audience knows exactly what they're getting. Here are some examples of ultra-specific headlines:

- The 3 weight lifting exercises you should never do more than once a week.
- 5 new software tools for professional social media marketers.
- The 10-step guide for establishing yourself as a travel writer.

4. **Urgent**. There is so much input in the world for humans to take in. And, thus, we are in constant competition for our reader's attention. The smart copywriter will build urgency into their headline—to compel the audience to perform the action. The urgency

factor forces the reader to consider our offer in the moment, rather than "putting it off till tomorrow"— when they'll forget all about us.

Among the Four *U*'s, this last one *"urgency"* is the trickiest to insert into your headlines. Here are some words that can help convey this emotion:

- quickly
- instantly
- finally
- at last
- alert

Using words like this adds a sense of hurriedness to the text. And employing this, in conjunction with the other Four U's, helps you come up with better headlines. Remember, the purpose of this formula is to provide your audience with useful, unique, urgent, and ultra-specific solutions to their problems. These are the types of headlines that tend to be most effective online.

Three Techniques for Rapid Headline-Generation

Now, to get your brain working, I'll list three of my favorite headline shortcuts below. These are the three "go-to techniques" you should consider, when you first sit down to do some copywriting.

Technique 1: Do a Brain-Dump

In this method, we sit down and generate as many appealing headlines as we can, as fast as we can. You can actually generate some good headlines in this "stream of consciousness" fashion. And you'll get a lot of bad headlines too. But the point is not to think about it too hard. We just want to get pen to paper, and brainstorm some headline ideas.

Here are a few examples I came up with:

- Headline 1: How to write good copy.
- Headline 2: How to write copy that increases sales.
- Headline 3: How this headline generates $10,000 every month.
- Headline 4: 3 copywriting tricks to double your sales.
- Headline 5: My all-time favorite formula for writing headlines.

Don't make it difficult. We simply want to get five to ten headlines down on paper, as fast as possible. And then, we sit back and choose the most appealing headline of the batch. And then ask yourself, how could I make this one headline better?

Technique 2: Look at product reviews from Amazon users

In this method, we can utilize Amazon to create great headlines. If you're selling a product in a niche on Amazon, then find your competing products and read their reviews. You'll notice that reviews on Amazon can receive "up votes" and "down votes."

So, look for the up-voted reviews and borrow ideas for your headlines from here.

An example of an Amazon review might be:

"I've read a lot of stuff about freelancing, but this guide answered my questions—in a complete system, step-by-step. It's the only guide I actually use. And it helped me get started on my freelance-writing career."

This is a nice Amazon review. And, we can derive nice headlines from this quote such as:

- This is the only freelancing guide you'll actually use!
- Follow this e-book step-by-step and get your first freelancing gig.
- A complete system—to start your freelance writing career the right way.

Technique 3: See which website is ranking on Google

A third shortcut, to come up with great headlines, is to simply analyze the headlines of the top 10 results on Google. Remember, Google's job is to display the search results that people want. If nobody clicks on these search results, then Google knows that the item was not what most people were looking for. Thus, you can think of Google as a contest—where the best headline wins (gets the most clicks).

There are other factors in Google ranking. So you don't necessarily always want to simply craft your headline based on the first search result of course. But get in the habit of reading the top website titles in your niche. Note the language they're using. You want to become intimately familiar with how these websites appeal to their customers, and how they use the jargon of their industry, to attract clicks.

What is a "Swipe File?"

Before we go much further, we have to learn what a "**swipe file**" is.

I hope the reader can appreciate the value in having an existing copywriting template (or formula) to follow. Just as working graphic designers almost *always* use existing photography or clipart for their ad creatives, working copywriters almost always start with a template, of some sort. Thankfully, consistently writing great ads doesn't require you to "create from scratch" each time you sit down to do a job. Instead, copywriters use templates often called "swipe files."

Similar to our formulaic example above, a "swipe file" is a collection of ad copy—containing already-proven text templates for headlines, content, and calls-to-action. When a copywriter needs inspiration, or when he gets *stuck* trying to produce unique copy, swipe files can be a godsend. The same copy that works in one business, often can work in another business, after just a few alterations. So having a thumbable list of successful ads at your fingertips is very useful.

As a good copywriter, you should make it part of your job, to constantly maintain a library of swipe files—throughout your career. Moreover, you should review these files repeatedly, such that their messages become a part of your brain—and referencing the tactics they capitalize upon, becomes second-nature.

No matter which industry you end up writing for, you should always be adding to your swipe file library. Here are some tips for gathering great swipe files:

- Browse the online platforms where your competitor's get most of their traffic. Look at his web advertisements, and take note of the ads that seem to be working for him. Take screenshots, and save them in a folder.
- Always pay attention to industry trends—particularly note what the big advertisers are writing in their ads this year.
- Take note of the ads that appear again and again, on your Facebook feeds, or on popular websites. If an ad is displaying often, this means that people are probably clicking on it.

Ch. 5: The Copy

In the previous chapter, we discussed the first part of a typical advertisement message—"the Headline." Now on to the next part—the ad copy itself.

Advertisement copy (often simply called "the copy"), typically refers to the main body of text below the ad's headline. Recall from the previous chapter, the role of the "ad headline," is to lure the reader in—so that he'll be curious enough to read-on. Once we've ensnared him with our headline, it is here, in this next body of text ("the copy") that we persuade our reader to consider what our product has to offer.

There is an art and a science to this endeavor, of course. And training to be a great copywriter takes years of practice. However, there are several key principles—that are timeless in their application. And that you should become intimately familiar with. We'll list these principles now:

Principle 1: Know your audience

How can you write compelling copy, if you don't know who you're trying to reach?

You can't.

So before you start writing, make sure you can answer the following questions:

- "Who you're writing for?"
- "What does your audience need?"
- "How does your audience think?"

You need to understand your target demographic to a tee. If you know them well, then you'll know what they're looking for, and what would inspire them to action.

To get in the right headspace, integrate a "buyer persona" in your copy. A "buyer persona" is a prototypical representation of your target customer—usually conceived using consumer studies, demographic research, or market experience.

To start creating a buyer persona, ask yourself a series of questions—that reveal her background and mode of living.

- What is her daily routine?
- What is her job?
- What ideas and goals does she have?
- What challenges is she facing?
- What are her shopping preferences?

Knowing these items about your target demographic, will reveal abundant and valuable insight—that you can use to generate copy more effectively.

Principle 2: Understand the difference between Product Features & Product Benefits

Before sitting down to write about your product, there are some questions (about your product), that you should be prepared to answer. Ask yourself:

1. What words will I be using, to grab my reader's attention?
2. What will cause my copy to "stand out" from the competing ads?
3. What are the benefits that my product offers, compared to others in my niche?
4. How will I know if I am succeeding in convincing my reader? What metric will I be tracking?

Take time to become familiar with the value your product has to offer your consumers. Describe your product's benefits using clear terms—and in such a way that your user is convinced that no other product is better than yours. The more benefits your product has, the more value it will provide to your customer.

Often, copywriters make the mistake of confusing the *features* of a product, with the *benefits* of the product. But there is a vast difference between features and benefits.

Features of a product are like the features of your face, such as your eyes, nose, and ears. But these features have benefits. For instance, the eyes allow you to see the colors of the world. The nose is for smelling. And your mouth is for tasting food.

Simply put:

- The **features** are the "product characteristics" that are designed into the product, and utilized to perform a function.
- And, the **benefits** of the product, are the value you garner from those functions.

A feature of your iPod is that it can store 10 Gigabytes of music on its internal disk drive. But the benefit is that you have instant access to your complete library of music, all in one pocket-sized box.

For a good exercise, it's often helpful to pull out a piece of paper and list all of your product's features on the left, and the benefits they produce on the right. As you're writing your ad copy, refer to this paper often, and try to put yourself in the head of someone who needs the benefits that your product is capable of providing. If you find yourself just rattling off product features like:

- 10x zoom lens,
- 20 gigabytes of storage,
- or antilock breaks

then, you're probably doing it wrong. Remember, the customer wants to know what benefit the features will bring him—not just about the features themselves.

Principle 3: Make your subjects feel special

Everybody loves to feel special and important. You should learn to exploit this psychological phenomenon in your copy. We want to selectively isolate our audience—in a good way—by telling them that they have been "hand-selected," and make them feel as if they are part of an exclusive bunch.

Speak to your audience directly and demonstrate an intimate understanding of their problem. Never speak down to them. Instead, understand that your audience is looking for a way to solve their own problem—in a unique, and fast fashion. So *relate* to them. And guide them through the buying process.

Principle 4: Add a touch of emotion

Two elements play a significant role in boosting sales—one is logic, and the other is emotion. Along with its other appealing attributes, the copy for your product should be thought-provoking, and connect to your target prospect, on an emotional level.

This is the reason why good commercials (and powerful marketing presentations) often make you laugh or cry. These displays create emotional moments, which have been shown to drive businesses. So, hopefully your copy will leave a mark on your audience's heart and mind. Particularly when your aim is to convert your prospects, into *long-lasting* clients.

Principle 5. Tell a story

Many advertisements grab their viewers' attention (and persuade them to purchase) via storytelling. Storytelling is a powerful tool in marketing and advertising—because people love to hear an exciting story that incites emotion. Invoking this phenomenon in your online copy is a powerful way to make your target prospect associate a positive "feeling" with your product.

Hit all the senses of your mark—by describing how he or she will feel (or look) with your product. A typical example of this is when luxury brands beautifully depict the status and exclusivity of their products. Painting a picture of your product (via good story-telling) will help your consumer connect with the product, and convince them to buy.

Principle 6: Know your medium

Once you know who you're writing for, and the type of response you can expect, take a moment to identify the *channel* and the *medium*—through which you will spread your advertising message.

This is essential to understand *before* moving on to writing your copy. But, before telling you the reason *why*, first, let's get to the definition of medium and channel.

- A **medium** is like a pipe through which your copy passes. Examples include newsprint, radio, or online web advertising.
- A **channel** is the environment or platform in which your target prospect receives your copy—such as via social media, news websites, or mobile devices.

Understanding the channel and medium is important, because this adds an element of specificity to the copy.

Think about it in this way—writing copy for radio is different than writing copy for an Instagram post, which is different than writing copy for a website landing page, which is different than writing copy in an email message, etc. The approach you use in each domain is altered by the domain itself.

So remain cognizant of your medium and channel throughout the copywriting process. Specifically, understand that people are of different states of mind and attention-levels, as they digest the information. For example, the advertisement copy that you would write for a public Talk Radio program, is different than the copy you would put on website pitch page.

Principle 7: Don't write dull or confusing copy

People don't pay attention to copy that's not appealing or useful. Ultimately, it is the value you offer, that determines your business success. This applies to copywriting as well. Avoid ethereal commentary, or existential banter. Instead, work hard to succinctly and clearly transpose the "value of your product," into clear and compelling words.

Principle 8: Utilize the power of words

Words hold an incredible amount of power. And, it's important to be aware of this power—every time you sit down to write.

Synonyms might convey similar meanings, but their psychological influence may be entirely different. For example, take the words *sad* and *devastated*, and think about the difference between them. The word "devastated" is a weightier term—and denotes more than mere daily melancholy.

Such powerful emotions can come packaged with words. And, when used right, they prompt the reader to be eager, curious, or excited to know more.

Here is a list of some powerful words—that you can use in your headlines and copy:

- sensational
- hurry
- wanted
- challenge
- help
- miracle
- startling
- remarkable
- amazing

Here are some words that encourage inclusion:

- Join
- Come along
- Become a member
- Become an insider
- Be one of the few

Here are some phrases that imply exclusivity:

- Exclusive offers

- Be our beta tester
- Only for members
- Available to subscribers only
- By invitation only
- Get it before everyone else

Principle 9: Tell them why they should listen to you

You have to give people a reason to listen to your message.

To accomplish this, copywriters will often appeal to authority, appeal to research data, or rely on celebrity endorsements. As you're writing your copy, put yourself in the reader's shoes, and keep asking yourself:

- Why should people follow what I'm saying?
- Why should they listen to me?
- Why should people take my suggestion?
- How will my product make people happier or healthier?
- How will my copy make people more interested in my offer?
- Which common or complex problems will my copy solve, or help to avoid?

Principle 10. Write for one target prospect

Ultimately, we are writing for one person. Not for a group or a crowd.

Therefore, add a personal touch to the copy by speaking about the wants, desires, and problems of one target prospect. Make that person feel special by referring to him as if you've known him for a long time, and you know exactly where he's coming from.

Principle 11. Always break up your copy

Never publish a "wall of text." A "wall of text" is a paragraph of copy, that merely contains words—without line breaks, bold text, italics, or bullet points. This is no fun for readers. Readers like their text to be broken up in logical clusters. Highlight (or bold) important words. And use an interesting font when appropriate.

Use short and concise sentences. Writing short lines doesn't mean losing information about your product. If you want your copywriting to sell, then you must write all your most essential benefits smartly and in small chunks.

While writing, always imagine that your reader is in a hurry. What would someone in a hurry read? A vast wall of text that looks like it comes out of a college biology textbook?

No.

Your message must be contained in copy that is light and readily-digestible. Small chunks of text make it easy for your customers to navigate through your words, and get the most out of the information—in the least amount of time.

Principle 12. Create a sense of urgency

Selling with copy is all about changing a person's mind about a product—from "I must have that" to "I must have that right now."

As Charles Bukowski wrote "there's nothing worse than too late."

Humans are loss-averse creatures. And they hate to miss out on a good deal—particularly on things that they want the most. Capitalize upon this phenomenon with your copy—and push your audience towards the purchase.

Typically, on websites, this is done by adding an animated countdown. But, even in more traditional marketing, deadlines are often used, like "Sale ends Sunday," or "Only available on Black Friday."

In any case, always remember that creating a sense of urgency often spurs people to action.

Principle 13. Add credibility with facts and statistics

Facts and visual statistical data make your copy compelling, and add credibility to your content. Stating facts and stats (particularly interesting ones) are one of the best ways to gain the consumer's confidence. Inserting facts and stats will improve the authority of your copy, and will present you as an expert.

Principle 14. Build social proof

Suppose you're browsing for products online, and you come across two competing products.

- One product has thousands of positive reviews (from admiring fans).
- And the other product just launched yesterday (and has no reviews).

Which product do you think will get more sales today?

As we're all aware, the product with the most reviews usually wins. The brain has a preference—to follow the behavior of the crowd, in almost any circumstance. This is natural consumer behavior.

Website reviews and ratings are the ultimate form of online "social proof." Social proof is often considered the most powerful motivator in the buying decision. And, for new products, it can be the most difficult signal to obtain.

Typical forms of social proof in copy are:

- Customer Testimonials
- Case studies
- Starred ratings
- Certification badges
- Editor's Choice Awards
- Endorsement by doctors and medical professionals
- Endorsement by industry leaders.

Principle 15: Test your copy and keep what works

Effective copywriting doesn't come naturally to everyone. It is a creative exercise, which must be honed over time. But, eventually, you must release your ad, and see how it performs. And, it is here where copywriters often make the mistake of believing that they have written the greatest ad known to man, and that it is sure to rack up sales at any moment.

But don't fall into this trap. There is a cognitive bias called the IKEA Effect—in which consumers place a disproportionately high value on products they have just created. So, after hours of laborious writing, your brain will naturally value your written words more than it probably should.

The only true test of your ad copy, is if it actually succeeds in converting readers into customers.

In the past, marketing companies were often never quite sure how effective any given marketing message was. Even still, to this day, the effectiveness of adverts that appear in traditional media (like television and radio), can often only be measured via indirect means. But, thanks to the advent of online advertising metrics, measuring the conversion rate of a web ad is easier, and quite quantifiable.

Consequently, when one of your web adverts is not performing, there is a tendency to insist that the impetus of its failure comes from ancillary forces—like the poor quality of the traffic, or the offer. And, indeed, sometimes this is true. But be prepared to consider that the copy itself (yes your own little creation), might be the cause too.

Ch. 6. The Call-to-Action

In the previous chapters, we've discussed the ad's headline and copy. Now comes the third and final part of a typical ad framework: the "Call-to-Action."

Recall that the "Call-to-Action" is the piece of content at the end of your marketing message, which tells the reader (or viewer or listener), what you want him to do next. As with everything else in copywriting, the nature of the Call-to-Action will be dependent upon the medium that you're writing in.

- If your ad is broadcasted over **radio**, then the Call-to-Action might be a phone number that you'd like the listener to call.

- If you're writing an **email**, then the Call-to-Action is usually a link—that you'd like the reader to click.

- If your copy is on a **website** pitch page, then your Call-to-Action is often a button on the page—that leads to a web form of some sort.

Whatever medium you choose, the underlying principles of the Call-to-Action are the same. It's the last step—where we ask our audience to make a decision regarding our offer. If you have been successful in keeping your target interested in your product thus far, then the Call-to-Action is where he decides to "pull the trigger." This often entails buying a product. But, may be something as simple as sharing a Link on Twitter, or (perhaps most common these days) typing his email address into our email opt-in box.

In any case, we've listed some Call-to-Action principles below.

Principle 1: Make the choices clear

The internet is a complicated place. And when you present people with too many choices, then it's easy for them to become anxious, annoyed, and confused.

On any given advert, you may have multiple ways to convert a reader. Particularly when it comes to webpage copy, there may be dozens of ways to convert a user on one page.

- You may sell dozens of products.
- You may have ten social media share buttons.
- You may have multiple email boxes—whizzing around your screen.

It's easy to cause information overload, and scare your reader away.

So, when you're crafting your Call-to-Action, try to limit the user's choices down to between one and three options. Typically, you want the user to:

- Call this phone number.
- Click this link to learn more.

- Click here to download.
- Click here to Add to Cart.

These are the typical Calls-to-Action that we're all familiar with. Your reader is too. And you make his decision process as effortless as possible, by keeping your Call-to-Action conspicuous and familiar.

Principle 2: Scarcity is powerful

Have you ever been considering the purchase of a product on Amazon or eBay, and noticed that little snippet of red text, that reads: "Hurry, only 3 items left!"

- How does that text make you feel?
- How would you feel if, just at the moment you decided to buy, someone else snatched your product first.

It's a horribly frustrating feeling, and we've all been there.

Scarcity, and the fear of missing out, is a powerful trigger in the human psyche. This is why you seem so many Call-to-Actions that feature such tricks. Typically, they'll be presented next to a meter—which tells us how many products are left. Or, an animated countdown clock, which shows us how much time we have to buy (before the clock runs out).

Whether these devices are real or contrived, often doesn't matter. They work to trick our brains into taking action—which is what the copywriter wants us to do.

Principle 3: Offer a "Free Bonus"

Have you ever watched those late-night TV infomercials, and wondered why they keep throwing in additional "bonus items?"

- "Buy the Widget-9000 mop and get a free plastic bucket."
- "Buy the Expresso-500 coffee maker, and get a free coffee cup."

For whatever reason, adding on additional bonus to products in your Call-to-Action often works. And may be the final tidbit of persuasion that pushes your reader over the edge.

Principle 4: Use "light profanity"

Some research has shown that carefully inserting light profanity in a Call-to-Action drives more sales. For example, the sentence "Act now, because this is a pretty damn good deal," contains the word "damn" and catches the reader off-guard a bit.

This is a product dependent trick of course. (You'd probably never use profanity on an ad for diamond rings.) But it can be useful on other (male-dominated) products, like electronics and stereo equipment.

Principle 5: Don't forget the Call-to-Action

You may be surprised to learn that the most common mistake we see in copywriting (and especially in content writing) is when the writer simply neglects to include any sort of Call-to-Action at all.

- Ask yourself how many times in your life you've found yourself scrolling down a webpage, only to reach the bottom, and then, not really knowing what you were supposed to click on next.
- Ask yourself how many times you've been to a website, and then, ten minutes later, you still weren't quite sure what they were selling, nor if they were (or were not) selling anything at all.

Your Call-to-Action should clearly tell your audience what to do next. And, what they will get—if they follow your instructions.

Especially, in the online world, writers tend to be too vague with their Calls-to-Action. And leave their readers wondering what to click on next. As the great User Experience designer Richard Littauer likes to say, we should always:

"Design like the user is drunk."

Meaning that, "clarity and brevity" are of utmost importance when crafting your Call-to-Action. Ask yourself, "Would a drunk person know what to do after reading my copy?"

It's ok to be creative, but be straightforward and clear. Use few words (only the most essential ones), scrutinize over your word-choice, make every word count, and (most importantly) tell the user what you want him to do next.

Ch. 7: Copywriting for Emails

As many Internet Marketers will tell you, building an email list is typically touted as the best way to reach new (and existing) customers. When setup correctly, your email marketing arm can serve as an "automated selling machine"—that automatically, and continuously feeds your customers information about your products.

Compelling email marketing, begins with attracting the right audience, and understanding what writing style triggers the best response from them. Email messages are much more intimate and targeted than traditional advertising, so you can adopt a more friendly and personal tone throughout your message.

The "Subject Field" is the "Headline"

Copywriting for an email list starts with the headline. All of the same headline-generation principles we've discussed in previous chapters, apply to the email headline too. But, with email, the headline is not some bold text—placed atop a page. Instead, for email marketing, the headline is actually the email's "subject field."

The subject field is the first bit of text that the user will see in his email app—when you send him a message. This is the first sentence he'll glance at—before deciding to open your message or not.

The Power of Focus

One of the most important characteristics of email marketing lies in understanding how the message is perceived, and how this interaction is different, than the other ways people communicate.

Have you ever been at work, and had a colleague send you an email with 10 different questions on it? Have you noticed that it can be difficult to address multiple points in a single email? That's because email works best when it is conveying one or two ideas. And not much more than that.

This applies to marketing emails too. Remember, your email will fall into the inbox of a busy person, who has already received 30 other emails that day. So if your email content consists of a long product catalog—detailing every feature for all 900 products offered by your company, then this email will simply be deleted.

Instead, before you send your email, ask yourself, "What is the one important action that I'd like this user to do today?"

That action might be:

- To read the email and learn about your Black Friday Sale coupon.
- To be notified of the launch of your new software app.
- Or, to be offered a coupon code for a future purchase.

What's important is that we focus our content, and compose our emails with one important action in mind.

It is better to send multiple emails over many months, than to send just one email—and attempt to cram in every marketing message that your company has ever produced.

The Deadline

The typical goal in email marketing, is to compel your email subscriber to perform an action—usually in the moment just after he's read your email content. You facilitate this process, and encourage your readers to "click that link" when you invoke some sort of time-constraint in your emails.

In the real world, every coupon and every sale has an expiration date—whether it's explicitly printed on the coupon or not. So, in your emails, be sure to constantly and consistently remind the user that "this offer won't last forever."

Typically, when a big sale is on, marketers will send a series of emails—each referencing the "last day of the sale." Most importantly, the smart marketer will put an indication in the copy, of the amount of time still remaining in the sale. For example, a typical "countdown email" might say:

- "There's just 3 days left in the big Christmas sale."
- "We'll be ending this sale at midnight on New Year's Eve."
- "The Back to School sale ends next Monday!"

So, whatever your offer may be, try to instill some sense of urgency, to coax the reader into clicking. And consider mentioning this impending deadline in the email copy as well as in the email's subject field. Remember, scarcity is a powerful trigger.

The Postscript

At the bottom of your email, seriously consider adding a postscript (or p.s.). As several notable email marketers have noted, people tend to read the first sentence and the last sentence of your email. And when you insert a postscript, it tends to draw the eye toward the bottom of the email canvas.

So, consider adding the most important bit of information here. Often, the postscript area is used for an opportunity to convey urgency. For example, you might write:

- P.S. This is the biggest discount we've ever offered, and the sale will end on Tuesday.
- P.S. We'll be removing this sales page next week, so check it out now.

Or, you might use the postscript area as a way to curtail anxiety and indecision. Like:

- P.S. This software does indeed work on both PC and Mac.
- P.S. You get 30 days to refund the product if you don't like it.

Postscripts have been shown to increase buyer clicks and lead to more user engagement.

The Valediction (or Closing Signature)

When it's finally time to end your email, it's best to sign out with your name or pen name. We want to remind your subscribers of two things—who you are, and what you sell.

Most people, who subscribe to your email list, will not read every single email you produce. They may have subscribed months ago (often years ago). And when they finally do get around to clicking on one of your emails, they may have no idea who you are. But, this doesn't mean they won't buy something from you. Quite the contrary. Sometimes people will remain dormant (and uninterested) on an email list for years, before a random message jogs their attention, and turns them into a paying customer. So it's typically helpful to sign your email with some sort of recognizable name and perhaps a company tagline—to remind your subscribers what you provide. Typical examples include:

- Peter Holland – Professional Auto Repair
- Kerry Underwood – Owner of Toronto Video Productions
- Jim Peterson – CEO of PoolAndSpa.com

Notice how, in these three examples, it's clear who we're talking to, and what their line of work is. This conspicuousness is important online.

Writing Compelling Email Newsletters

Not all email messages are designed to sell something—at least not right away. Instead, many websites use their email list as a "newsletter"—to notify a group of subscribers about products or events they may be interested in.

The famous news website DrudgeReport.com currently receives three million page visits per day, but was originally started as a simple email-based newsletter—written and sent from Matt Drudge's apartment in Hollywood, California.

So what sort of content can we put into our email newsletters, to make them as engaging as Drudge's?

Well, first let's describe what content we do not want to include.

First off, the most financially successful email newsletters tend to be extremely simple. Just black text on a white background. Flashy emails, piled with product information, irrelevant graphics, and gaudy promotions, tend to confuse users. And can be off-putting.

- Think of what the emails you normally respond to look like?
- What does an email from your best friend look like?
- Does your friend include fancy banners and graphics in his email content?

Typically not.

Remember, email marketing works best when it's simple and intimate. Think of each of your subscribers as your friend. Why? Because we want to make your email subscribers feel as if they are talking to a friend. Ideally, they'll pay attention to what you are doing, and will become excited about receiving your messages.

The body of your newsletter copy should have a personal touch. It should be a combination of great content and storytelling. And, take some time to ask your reader about their opinion too!

Try to become the person that they love listening to. This is easy to accomplish if the product or service you're selling actually does provide real value to their lives. Give your subscribers something they can take advantage of, and show them how they can use what you're offering.

Topics for Email Newsletters

To maintain your engagement with your subscribers, it's often best to discuss new and novel topics. This can be a challenging task to maintain, particularly if you've been writing about the same subject for years.

But, here are a few tips, to churn out new ideas consistently.

1. Create a journal or keep a log, of every newsletter topic you've created for your subscribers. Preferably, you'll keep each email file in an app that allows you to very easily flip through each message—in chronological order. This is useful, because it prevents you from becoming a broken record—and sending the same message, again and again.

2. You can get novel ideas in Google by using the "People Also Ask" or the "Google Related Searches" functions on the Google search engine results page. These areas

are designed to show you what other people (like you) are also wondering about. Thus, they almost always contain relevant information. So, as you type in queries (related to your niche), pay attention to these other areas on google, and look to see if any ancillary topics catch your eye.

3. Use social media platforms like Reddit and Quora, to find topics that other people in your niche are wondering about. These websites are usually a flurry of activity and you can find someone asking a question in almost every topic imaginable.

4. A popular formula for creating Email Newsletter content is *life* + *subject* = *email newsletter*. In this formula, the word *life* refers to the regular everyday things that happen in your life (typically with family, kids, and friends). And, the word *subject* refers to the topic you wish to educate your subscribers about. For example, you might start off your email talking about how you've been having trouble getting your baby to sleep through the night. And then mention how your baby-monitoring product has helped you to check up on your child without disturbing his sleep. The goal is, to give your subscribers a message that they can relate to, and to display the benefits of your product or service to them, in a casual way.

5. Speak directly to your subscribers. Try to avoid the word "we" and use the words "I" and "you" more. This will make your subscriber feel directly engaged in the

conversation. And, she may be more likely to read your email content.

6. Help more, and sell less. People don't like to be pitched to in personal emails. But they do (indeed) want valuable information—that will solve their problems. So, when you're writing copy for your newsletter, try to make at least 80% of your content about useful and causal information. And avoid self-promotion or product sales. Too much self-promotion will turn your subscribers off, and might get them to unsubscribe.

7. Appreciate the power of brevity. Remember, most people don't have time to read a long email. So don't fill it with too much information. If you've got a lot to tell your subscribers, then format your email with multiple headlines, or consider linking directly to a website pitch page or YouTube video.

The Email Opt-in Box

In any discussion of email copywriting, there is one topic that is consistently neglected. Copywriters will write reams of text about the email itself. But they often forget the most important part— the copy for the email opt-in box.

For those who have never worked with email lists, the "email opt-in box" is that little box on your website which prompts your web visitor for his email address. Typically it will consist of an email address field, a Submit button, and some copy that tells the user why he should give you his email address.

Don't make the mistake of ignoring the copywriting in this area. For, indeed, many companies live and die based solely upon how many email addresses they are able to gather. So the words you write in your email opt-in box, may actually be more important than the words in your email itself.

With that said, let's list some rules for proper opt-in box copywriting.

Rule 1: Keep your opt-in form simple

Keep your opt-in form as simple as possible. The most common mistake we see on websites is forms that contain too many text fields. For a general rule of thumb:

> As the number of text fields in your opt-in form increases, the number of users who will submit the opt-in form decreases.

People don't like to fill out forms. Forms are tedious, tiresome, mentally taxing, and we all hate them. So, ideally, your form will only have two inputs—a field for the user's email address, and the submit button itself. That's it.

This is not always possible on some websites of course. For example, if you're collecting data for a credit background check, or an insurance application, then one field probably won't work. But for most online and ecommerce businesses, merely getting the user's email address is fine.

Rule 2: Make your opt-in form easy to find

Most websites make the mistake of either making the opt-in form too difficult to find, or of slamming it in front of the user's face every ten seconds. Ideally, you'll find a middle ground someplace. Typically, static opt-in forms work best when they are placed in the top-right corner of each page of your blog, and at the bottom of every blog post.

You can use popout opt-in forms as well. And these do get higher conversion rates. But just be warned that they tend to annoy users. And if your form pops up more than once, you may scare them away.

Rule 3: Your user must know why he's signing up

Unfortunately, most websites do not give their visitors a reason to signup to their email list. The extent of their opt-in box copywriting might be one sentence, which exclaims:

"Subscribe to our newsletter!"

As should be obvious, to a new website visitor, this sentence is not very compelling. With email opt-in boxes, it's important that the user be made aware of exactly what *immediate benefit* he will get, after surrendering his email address.

- Will he get a coupon after he signs up?
- Will he get a free printable map of Hollywood?
- Will he get access to a private consulting call?

If you want new visitors to sign up, you need to make the incentive crystal clear. And, indeed, there must always be an incentive of some sort. Typically, website owners use free informational giveaways, of one form or another. This might be a downloadable PDF, image, or some other sort of digital resource.

In any case, just be cognizant of the fact that people usually need a reason to perform an action. Your copy should be readily able to answer that *most important of customer questions*:

"What's in it for me?"

Rule 4: Use social proof

As with every other aspect of human-interaction, social proof is (consistently) one of the most powerful motivators. So it's useful to use this trigger in your opt-in box copy as well. Try one of the following blurbs of text below your submit button:

- Tell your user how many other people have already signed up for your email list. For example, say "Over 9,000 people have already signed up!"
- Or, try displaying a customer testimonial below the button. This works best when you show an image of a happy customer's face, and a text balloon—featuring a quote from him—saying something like, "This content enabled me to triple my growth last quarter."

Such examples of social proof advertise authority, and indicate that your email list is worth signing up to.

Rule 5: Give your prospects a way out

People don't like to make the wrong decision. In the moments before the brain engages in an action, it is presented with a moment of doubt. A flurry of anxiety rushes across your cortex, and you find yourself wondering, "Should I really be doing this?"

As copywriters, we can alleviate this stress by offering a reassuring bit of text below the action point. Have you ever wondered why so many television infomercials exclaim: "You can cancel any time!" or "30-day money back guarantee!" Well, this is why.

So, consider ending your opt-in box with the sentence saying something like:

"You can unsubscribe at any time."

Such proclamations make your customer feel safe, and gives him the security of a hypothetical magic parachute.

Ch. 8: How to keep your Emails out of Junk Mail

One of the most challenging aspect of email marketing is just keeping your emails out of the Junk Mail folder itself. Nobody is going to read your marketing email content, if they never actually receive your email. So, we thought it wise to include a chapter here about how the email gods determine which emails are worthy of the inbox, and which emails go straight to junk mail, or (more recently) to the "Gmail Promotions" folder.

The algorithms that perform the chore of email sorting are complicated, ever-changing, and, are top-secret information. The Gmail programmers are not going to tell anyone how their spam filters work of course. However, via a whole lot of experimentation (and after sending many, many emails), we have a pretty good idea about which factors are at play.

Below, we've listed these factors. Understand that any given one of these attributes should not be considered by itself. Rather, the decision to disregard any given email message, is probably based on a composite analysis—of a cocktail of factors. With that said, while we can never fully know how the filters work, if you can avoid the following pitfalls in your marketing campaign, you'll most likely have a higher click-through-rate than your competitors.

Factor 1: Which email provider is your customer using?

We've mentioned Gmail several times in this book because Gmail holds the biggest email market share at 53%. Yahoo and Outlook are a distant second and third. These stats will vary from niche to niche. But chances are, if you have a company email list, then half of your subscribers will be on Gmail.

Because of this fact, email marketers tend to focus on the particular message-processing behavior of Gmail, over the other email providers. But just be aware, that every provider uses their own system of course. The same email you send might be readily received on Yahoo, but rejected on Gmail.

Factor 2: Is the email coming from a "dirty server?"

One of the most important spam filters is based on the history of the server that's sending the email. Every email provider maintains a list of "good and bad" email servers. A bad email server, is a computer that does nothing but spit out spam email, all day and night—typically trying to sell you Viagra pills, or banking scams from the Nigerian Consulate. Because every computer on the internet has its own unique IP address, it's rather easy for email providers to simply keep a log of such malevolent servers. And then, when they receive an email from one of these servers, they simply flag it, and send it straight to your junk mail folder—so it doesn't bother you.

Now, some servers are dirtier than others. So this enterprise is not so black and white. But, in any case, perhaps the best way to avoid this conflict, is to use a reputable company to host your subscriber list and send your emails. Good autoresponders take their server IP addresses seriously. And they work hard to try to prevent their servers from being blacklisted as a "spam" server.

So, if you're looking for an email provider, it's best to go with a reputable company. Aweber, MailChimp, iContact, InfusionSoft are four of the big names in email right now.

Factor 3: Has the user replied to you before?

Gmail maintains a history of interaction with every email. So, if you can get the user to reply to one of your emails, then the next email you send him, has a higher chance of getting through to him.

Gmail knows that, if the user keeps replying to an email address, then that email address probably has value to him. So it makes sense for them to make sure that all future emails from this address get through.

Factor 4: Has the user clicked your email links before?

Remember, in email marketing the Call-to-Action is the link itself, that we place at various points in our email messages. If a user has a history of clicking links (contained in the emails you send him), then it can be assumed that the user is getting value from your links. So getting a high CTR (Click-Through Rate) probably helps you get past the spam filters too.

Factor 5: Have other Gmail users clicked the SPAM button on your email?

When you're using Gmail, look up at the top row of buttons in the interface, and spot the little grey exclamation mark that reads, "Report Spam." When you push this button, you immediately tag the open email message as spam. But, not only does Gmail get rid of it for you, they also make a note in their own spam log.

Remember, 53% of your email recipients will be using Gmail. So suppose that you send an email out on Monday morning to 100 people. The expectation is that 53 of these people will be using Gmail. Now suppose that, of this set of 53 users, the first 10 people who opened your email message, didn't like it. And they clicked the grey Report Spam button.

So, when the next 10 people login to check their email, Google already knows that the previous 10 people didn't like it. This probably affects the way Google sorts this email, as well as any future email you send that week. Google is using this "wisdom of crowds" system to let the crowd dictate what is "spam," and what is not.

So, whatever you do, don't produce low-quality emails, that people are prone to think of as "spammy." Because, even if it's not, it might be perceived that way. And that can affect your future email campaigns.

Factor 6: Does the email have any tracking codes in it?

When real people send email to each other, they don't put tracking codes in it. But autoresponder services do. Unfortunately, tracking codes are often considered necessary, for gauging how effective an email campaign is.

Without tracking codes, it's difficult to know how many people are opening your email messages, or clicking on your links. But with tracking codes, your email could get flagged for spam.

Now, the trigger is not so simple of course. Tracking codes are only one factor, and, compared to the other factors we discussed in this book, they are most likely a minor one.

Factor 7: Has this email already been seen today?

Gmail doesn't like it when their user receives the same message again and again. So if you're sending the exact same email, at various times throughout the day, it's probably a bad sign. Moreover, if you compose a long email, but then only change a sentence or two, then this too is probably enough to invoke their wrath.

So, always send unique content to your email subscribers.

Factor 8: Is the email content too light?

We've done our own experiments using email consisting of just two or three sentences, and emails that contain longish content—using business-like language. The long emails tend to get rejected less than the short emails—especially those that have a "business casual" tone.

This is a generalization of course. Sometimes short emails are warranted. But, when you're considering your email length, it's typically best to aim for over 150 words. And avoid misspellings and grammar mistakes.

Factor 9: Does the email contain "salesy" words?

Some email content is easily spotted as sounding too "spammy" or "salesy" (by both man and machine). Such emails may contain words like:

- Buy Now
- Coupon
- Black Friday Sale
- Discount
- Etc.

These words indicate that you're trying to sell something. And, indeed, that is (of course) the point of email marketing. So, in the final days of an email marketing campaign, using such words is probably unavoidable.

But just remain cognizant of the types of words you use in your messages—particularly in your "pre-sale content emails"—which are mostly about "warming up" an audience—before the actual sale starts.

Wrapping up

Ultimately, the Gmail algorithm considers all of the above-described factors (and probably many, many more) when it decides how to route your email. We'll never know all the underlying mechanics of this process, so don't spend too much time attempting to unearth it, or "game" Google. That's a game you can't win.

Instead, work hard to write content that is pleasing to your readers, and provides them with valuable products, that they do indeed need. When your email marketing efforts (and message), is congruous with the interests of your email subscribers, then there is little need to worry about the triggers we've specified here. Because, your users will naturally interact with your email links and content. And this will ward off the critical eye of the Gmail algorithms.

Ch. 9: When Copywriting meets User Interface Design

In this chapter, we'll talk about the exciting, emerging field of User Interface design. Traditionally, "copywriters of old" never had to concern themselves with such technical matters. They would write the copy, and simply hand it off to the printers.

But, these days (as you've probably noticed), if you're selling something, then you're probably selling it online. And that means, the copy you write, will (almost always) be placed on a webpage somewhere. Moreover, because so many working copywriters also have their own websites or online stores (as a side gig or even as a full time job), then you will (most likely) deal with webpage textual layout issues at some point. So, it's valuable to have some degree of technical knowledge in this field.

What is User Interface Design?

So, what is User Interface Design?

Whenever you push a button, turn a knob, or flip a switch, you are interacting with an interface. And behind this interface, somebody (somewhere out there in the world), at some point, had to sit down and design it.

They had to make decisions like:

- What color should the switch be?
- When should I use a button instead of a knob?
- What sort of sound should I use for this button?
- What text should I write along the top of the device?

At first glance, these might seem like trivial questions. But, actually, they can be a matter of life and death—particularly when it comes to airplane control panels, industrial equipment, or medical devices. Yet, most people are not even aware that this field of study even exists!

This is possibly due to the fact that Interface Design industry has many names:

- Back in the day, User Interface Design was often called "MMI" (**Man Machine Interaction**). But that name was a bit too sexist…
- So they started calling it HMI (**Human-Machine Interaction**). Which is a bit confusing because sometimes when people say HMI they're referring to the interface device itself—sometimes HMI means **Human-Machine *Interface***.
- But then came the advent of personal computing— computers are not typically referred to as "machines" anymore. So they changed the "M" to a "C." (**Human-**

Computer Interaction) People who specialize in software interfaces or web interfaces might use this term. But the populous hadn't adopted technology to the degree that it has today, and this term "HCI" is more of an academic term.

- The most commonly used term these days is probably just UI (which stands for "**User Interface**." And this is often paired with the word "Design" as in "**User Interface Design**"). And this is often paired with the acronym "UX" which means "**User Experience**."

- Quite often, these two acronyms are placed side-by-side. Usually written as **UI/UX** (User Interface Design / User Experience Design). (For right or wrong, these words are often used interchangeably in the industry.)

In any case, it doesn't really matter what you call it. These are all just fancy words that describe the process of obtaining our desired goal. Which is to:

Make the user happy!

I.e. when we design an interface or write copy for a website, we strive to make the user's chore (of learning what our product is and how to buy it) as effortless as possible.

- We don't want to confuse the user.
- We don't make buttons hard to find.
- We don't make our text too small, or too big.
- We don't tell him things he doesn't need to know.
- We don't make useless information popup in front of his face repeatedly.

In other words, we try not to piss our user off!

Our objective is nicely summed up in the title of interface designer Steve Krug's book entitled:

"Don't Make Me Think."

That's exactly it.

Ideally, the user's experience will be so intuitive, that conscious thought will not even be required of him.

The original edition of "Don't Make Me Think" was published over 15 years ago, and is a bit dated now. But it's easily the most widely-read book in this field of Interface Design. And, it's worth reading the updated version if you get a chance. Because it's an excellent introduction to User Interface Design.

No technical training required.

Non-technical readers need not be intimidated by the technicalities of our discussion here. We're not talking about teaching you to be a programmer. Rather, for our purposes here, we're mostly concerned with how text, buttons, and links are laid out on a webpage. Indeed, if you can only get these three components right, then the rest of the widgets and gizmos you put on your website are largely irrelevant.

Additionally, you may be surprised to learn that programmers and web designers are often much worse at UI design than the copywriters are. Why? Because they were never taught to build webpages that sell products to humans. Rather, programmers and web designers think in terms of algorithms, and HTML elements. And they often find it difficult to see their website from the perspective of a new user.

This may sound counterintuitive, but as you get more into User Interface Design, you'll be continuously dumbfounded by the design choices that (otherwise technically-capable developers) often make.-

Let's do a UI Job

So now, let's do a User Interface Design job. For this exercise, we're going to be fixing up the webpage for the software company VMWare. They sell a software app called Fusion 7. And their pitch page is pretty bad.

Take a look at Figure A.

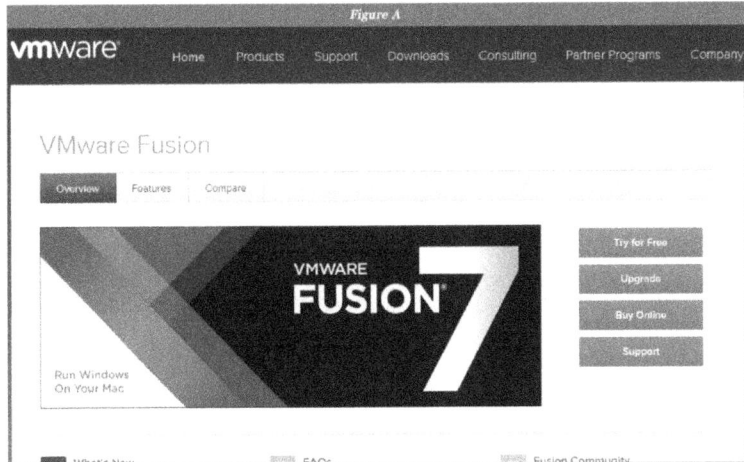

Figure A

This is a screenshot of the Fusion 7 webpage, taken "above the fold." The term "above the fold" is an old copywriting term that refers to the content above the fold of a newspaper. Obviously, the text on the top-first page of a newspaper is the most important text in the entire paper. (This is the text that people see as they're walking by the newsstand.)

In the digital world, the term "above the fold" refers to the content at the top of the website. This is the content you see when you first visit a website with your web browser—and before you scroll down the page. (Thankfully, VMware has made some improvements to their webpage in recent years. But this is what the page looked like for version 7 of their product.)

So, in glancing at this image, ask yourself how we could make this webpage better? Or, how could we change the copy and layout of this page, such that it will sell more units?

The Frank Kern Shortcut

The easiest way to tackle this question, is to start with a copywriting shortcut I learned from the famous Internet Marketer Frank Kern—who (reportedly) learned this trick from an old boss he worked for.

The trick goes like this:

When you're writing copy, you should be able to quickly convey three foundational points to your target consumer:

1. This is what I got.
2. This is what it will do for you.
3. This is what I want you to do next.

> If your website visitor is not able to answer these three questions, within five seconds of landing on your page, then you're probably doing something wrong!

Remember, the internet is a strange and complicated place. When we're trying to get someone to buy something online, we have to make everything easy for him. And, surprisingly, as you browse websites online, you'll find that (for the majority of websites) it's often very difficult to answer these three simple questions.

What's wrong with this website?

So, with our Frank Kern heuristic in mind, stare at our webpage image again, and ask yourself:

- "What is this webpage trying to sell me?"
- "Why does this webpage even exist?"

Try to put yourself in the shoes of a new user.

- Imagine you're seeing this webpage for this first time.
- Imagine you're sitting in a busy, noisy office.
- Imagine you have a thousand other things to do today.
- Imagine you have to pick up your kids from school in 15 minutes.
- Imagine you're distracted by music blaring from your kid's room.

With all the distractions of everyday life, would you be able to determine what this page is about?

What pieces of information could someone really come to know, after glancing at this webpage?

All we know is:

1. There's something on this webpage called Vmware.
2. There's something here called Fusion.
3. And, the number 7 has something to do with... something...

So, ask yourself:

- Do you find any of this information to be of particular importance to you?
- Are these three pieces of information (in any way), prompting you to buy anything from this company?
- Do you know what this product even does?
- Can you even tell if this company is selling a product or not?

I remember, when I first came to this webpage, it took me a while to figure out what they were trying to tell me. And the reason is pretty clear. Because it's hard to know what this product "VMware Fusion 7" actually does—unless you are observant enough to ignore everything on this page, except the tiny bit of grey text in the bottom-left corner, which reads:

"Run Windows on Your Mac."

Above the fold, this is the only useful datum of information on the entire webpage!

This is what Fusion 7 does. It allows you to run Microsoft Windows apps on your Apple Mac. But you'd never know that unless you were observant enough to locate the little grey text in the corner.

I hope it's obvious to you that this is not a very efficient layout— if you're trying to sell a complex software product to people over the internet.

Let's fix this website

Glance at Figure B, and let's talk about our new and improved design.

Figure B

Remember, as we've learned at the start of this book, the copywriter's job is broken down into three component parts.

1. The Headline
2. The Copy
3. The Call-to-Action

If you glance at the original version of the page in Figure A, you'll notice that the page does not have a well-defined representation of these three components at all. (Remember earlier when I said that web-developers are not very good at designing product web pages? This is why. Because they don't know how to write copy.)

So, with these three copywriting components in mind, let's talk about our improved webpage in Figure B.

Component 1: The Headline

First, notice all the dead white space along the top in Figure A. There's a lot of room here that I'd like to use. Because this is where (the most important copywriting element on a page) "the headline" should have been placed. But instead, the web designer merely wrote the words "VMware Fusion" here—and this text just doesn't mean anything to a new visitor.

So let's add a bold sentence for our headline. One that actually tells the user what this software is, and what this software does. Notice in Figure B, we wrote:

"Fusion 7 lets you run Windows on your Mac."

That's exactly what Fusion 7 does. If you buy Fusion 7, then you can run Microsoft Windows on your Mac. Notice how we're making our headline as blatantly conspicuous as possible—using a large orange font, and centering our text to the middle of the page.

Component 2: The Copy

Notice in Figure A, the web designer doesn't even have much copy on his page. Instead, he drew this big ugly rectangular image here. It's great to have a product graphic above-the-fold on your homepage. But this is just a stylized way of displaying the number seven—which just doesn't add anything to our pitch. Most users wouldn't even know what this number 7 even represents. (It represents the software's "current version number.") But who cares?

So, in our improved site in Figure B, we deleted the big ugly image. Then, we added a green sub-heading which reads:

Use all your favorite Microsoft Windows software inside your Apple Mac!

And, under our sub-heading, we wrote a paragraph of copy, that describes our product.

Component 3: The Call-To-Action

Typically, with software app pitch pages, the Call-to-Action contains three possible steps. The user can:

1. Click a button to download the free trial of the app.

2. Click a button to buy it now.
3. Click the video Play Button to watch a demo video and learn more.

We want the user to perform at least one of these three actions.

Notice how, in the original website (Figure A), the web designer mashed his Call-to-Action buttons between other innocuous blue buttons—like for Support and Upgrade. While it's great to have such buttons on your website, merging Support and Upgrade buttons with pitch page content is typically not desirable. So we minimized these two buttons, and changed them into links on our version in Figure B.

For our revised Call-to-Action area, we'll start form left to right.

1. On the left side, notice the green button that says "Download the Fusion 7 Free Trial." This is much more conspicuous than the blue button that sat on the top right corner. And since getting the free app trial into the user's hand is such a vital step in online software sales, we went with some multi-line text here for our button—that tells the user exactly what he's getting.
2. Next to that, we have an orange button that says "Buy Fusion 7." On the original website, this button was colored blue, and said "Buy Online." Remember, when it comes to crafting your text for a Call-to-Action, you have to tell the user exactly what a button does. The button label "Buy Fusion 7" has much more specificity than the button label "Buy Online." Additionally, we changed our button color from blue to orange—

because orange is the traditional color of commerce—often used for Buy Buttons online.

3. Finally, the third button in our Call-to-Action area is the red video Play Button. This website already has a wonderful software demo video. (It's got great animation, and it actually tells the user about the product features quite well.) But you'd never know it. Because they buried their video deep down in their website content. So in our Figure B, we moved this video up above the fold. Now you'll notice that we drew our own thumbnail image for our product video. Video thumbnails should attempt to represent the video content to the user. That's why we're showing a laptop running Windows and a Mac laptop, with an orange arrow between the two—indicating to the user that Fusion 7 lets you run Windows on your Mac.

Below our Call-to-Action we've placed our "Upgrade" and "Support" links for existing customers. Note that an existing customer, is a much different animal than a new user—who merely stumbles upon your website randomly from Google.

Existing customers have already bought something from you. Money has already been exchanged. So, there typically isn't a pressing need to make the buttons they'd use so prevalent. Observe in the original website in Figure A how the web designer merged his buttons for existing customers, with his buttons for new customers. (e.g. the Buy Button is right near the Support button.) This is typically not desirable because, when it comes to your Call-to-Action, that sole intent should be to sell to new users. So merging these buttons together only confuses your organic incoming traffic.

Can we Complete Frank Kern's Points now?

In glancing at our new creation, let's see if Frank Kern's three points are (now) adequately conveyed to a target consumer. Recall, the criteria were:

1. This is what I got.
2. This is what it will do for you.
3. This is what I want you to do next.

So, in looking at our new webpage, can we answer these three questions easily now?

Just our new headline alone makes this task easier. It reads "Fusion 7 lets you run Windows on your Mac."

So let's fill in the blanks.

- This is what I got: "Fusion 7"
- This is what it will do for you: "Runs Microsoft Windows on your Mac."
- This is what I want you to do next: Recall our new Call-to-Action now has three possible buttons. "You can download the trial, buy it now, or watch the video to learn more."

Because of our new layout of components on our pitch page, it's much easier for a user to discern what this webpage is about, and what value we're offering him. All of our most important pitch components are now above the fold.

And, most importantly, we have incorporated the three key components of any sales letter: the Heading, the Copy, and the Call-to-Action.

You should always split-test pitch pages. But it is my opinion that, because of our revisions, this webpage would sell more software than the original webpage. And of course, that's the entire point. To sell more stuff. To increase conversions on our webpage.

In UI Design, very subtle changes can lead to big rewards. And, as you get more into this stuff, you'll find that it's typical of companies (even big companies) to make very obvious mistakes on their product webpages. Not because their employees aren't smart! (The guys at Vmware are very smart! It's extremely difficult to program complex software apps like Fusion7.) But the point is, User Interface Design is not about "smarts." Because these skillsets (User Interface Design / User Experience Design / Copywriting...), these skills are not dependent on raw intelligence, or programming ability, or graphic-design ability, or artistic talent. During our little fixup, I didn't program or draw anything on this webpage at all. Mostly I just manipulated the text and the button colors, and I moved stuff around on the page.

I want to stress that point. What people don't realize is that the mere positioning of your page elements, is often more important than the elements themselves. The way that your information is arranged on your interface is pivotal. It can mean the difference between getting a sale and not getting a sale. Between making your users happy, or just confusing them.

Doing website copywriting these days means making both your human users (and the Search Engine robots) happy.

The search engines ("Googlebot"), they're looking for things like:

- Descriptive Keywords, scattered throughout your content. (Are you referring to your product or service the same way that your customers do?)
- Conspicuous navigation (Are your pages easy to get to? Can Googlebot effortlessly crawl through and index your entire website with ease?)

But the human users (your customers) are looking for things like:

- Message clarity. Is the purpose of your webpage obvious to the user? Can he ascertain what you're trying to tell him?
- Content that reflects their search goals. Do you sell what he's looking for? If he typed in the keywords "How to build a dog house," and you're trying to sell him a camera, then your content obviously doesn't reflect his commercial intent.
- And, also an easy-to-use, attractive interface. Are your buttons clearly marked? Are the action steps you'd like the user to take next, obvious to him?

I hope you can see that a more holistic approach is desirable online. I'm trying to convey the importance of learning to see your web copy form both a human and a machine perspective. These days, it's best if you can do both. And if you know how to harmonize these skillsets, that's quite an asset to have in your copywriting toolbox.

Ch. 10: Copywriting for Websites

In the previous chapter, we discussed User Interface Design, and how web components should be arranged on your pitch page. Now, in this chapter, we'll talk more about the pitch page copy itself.

Website pitch page copy is typically presented as a long-form sales letter—which describes a product to your web visitor. The page might be trying to sell you a membership program, physical or digital product (such as an eBook or web class), or some other service.

User's typically land on your pitch page after following a link from Google, a Pay-per-click ad, or perhaps from a link in your marketing email. In either case, your pitch page is vitally important. Because it sits at the final step in the buyer's decision process.

Your website pitch page holds the almighty "Buy Button." And it is at this point where your visitor has to decide—to part with his money (and buy your product), or not.

So, obviously, as copywriters, it's important for us to get this page right.

Know your Audience

As with any type of web copy, before you sit down to write your pitch page content, you want to identify your audience. This can be tricky with pitch pages, because you may never be quite sure where your visitors are coming from.

- Perhaps your visitor just found your website via Google, and hence, this is the first time he's ever heard of your company.
- Or, perhaps your visitor has been following you for years, and is finally ready to buy.
- Or, perhaps your visitor is an industry professional, and he is fully aware of you and your competitors.

So, as you can see from the above examples, your website pitch page has to be versatile enough to accommodate potential buyers, who occupy varying points of the consumer spectrum.

With that said, we must always strive to be aware of our readers' wants and needs. Know the obstacles or problems they're facing, and work to provide them with a solution. As in our previous exercises, it's beneficial to generate a list of your product's benefits and features. Recall, that a feature is an attribute on your product that performs a function. And a benefit is the value your customer garners from this function. Your iPod's 10 Gigabytes of internal memory is a feature. But the benefit is that you can access your entire library of music from your pocket.

So, before writing your website pitch page, remain cognizant of your product's features and benefits, and rank-order them—so that you talk about the most important ones on the top of your pitch page.

It's also helpful to write down any objections that a potential customer might have. And then, describe how your product is not susceptible to his criticism. Or, if the customer does have a legitimate concern, acknowledge the issue, but tout the other virtues your product may have. Remember, nobody expects your product to be perfect. And people tend to value "honesty" over supposed "perfection" anyway.

Pitch Page Readers are Different...

As we've already expressed, the vast majority of readers will typically peruse (or skim) your advertisement copy. This is almost always true. However, when it comes to website pitch pages, this rule is sometimes broken.

Again, recall that your pitch page holds your "Buy Button." And your user has to eventually decide if he wants to click this button, or not. Clicking this button, might mean that your visitor is handing over hundreds (or often thousands) of dollars. Therefore, unlike casual readers (who are just glancing at your ads while playing on Facebook), "pitch page readers" may scroll up and down your page—reading your advertisement copy again, and again, and again. Why? Because:

- They're trying to convince themselves that you are indeed selling the answer to their problem.
- They're trying to convince themselves that they should trust you.
- They're trying to convince themselves that you are the one they should be giving their money to.

This is an important point to understand. The presence of the Buy Button on your pitch page, has a tendency to incite atypical user behavior—behavior that you wouldn't find on a typical advert.

So it's important to "cover all your bases" on pitch pages. And be sure that your message is sound, saleable, and consistent—from top to bottom.

Pitch Page Copywriting Principles

With the above in mind, let's review some general principles for composing your pitch page content.

Principle 1: Use a big and conspicuous headline

One of the most common copywriting problems that we see on web pitch pages, is that the writer often neglects to tell the reader exactly what he's selling. He'll craft a long and beautiful webpage—exclaiming the features of his product, and the bedazzling flurry of options that will be at the reader's fingertips—as soon as he clicks the Buy Button.

Unfortunately, website owners will often be so intimately familiar with their own product, that they'll find it difficult to see their website—from the perspective of a new visitor. And, humorously, they'll fail to tell the visitor exactly what they're selling.

This was a prevalent mistake in the Fusion 7 example in the previous chapter. It especially happens a lot with complex tech products or software apps and services. A pitch page will start off with an ambiguous title, such as:

The Super Widget 5000 has a 25 millisecond FPS with a dual-band T-splitter, and fiber-optic uplink.

Such headlines are almost always a bad idea (even if you're selling to industry professionals). Instead, write your pitch page headline using drop-dead simple language. Like this:

The WebCam 5000 lets you broadcast high-definition video—direct to your online fans.

Generally, in pitch page headlines, you want to describe exactly what your product can do for the reader, in one simple (easy-to-understand) sentence. A compelling top headline will persuade the reader, to make a decision about whether or not this is a product he's interested in. And it's the best way to engage the reader—as soon as he lands on your pitch page.

Principle 2: Set the tone

The tone of your pitch page should be familiar and effortless. Small paragraphs, and short sentences, are typically preferred. We want to grab the user's attention. Be creative, but use a simple lexicon—such that each sentence is easy to understand. Don't try to be too clever with the English language, or add fake information that your product can't accomplish.

Address your audience, using the words "you" and "I" a lot. Make your audience feel that you are talking directly to them.

Principle 3: Use subheadings (lots of subheadings)

Recall that pitch pages are "long-form sales letters." Meaning that they are typically content-heavy. And, when your visitors first arrive, they will often rapidly scroll up and down the page—to familiarize themselves with your pitch.

Because of this, subheadings are particularly important on pitch pages. Subheadings are headlines that define various independent sections of your pitch page content. And they can be used to callout important product features or benefits.

Unlike formatting for email copy or advert copy, pitch page copy will typically contain between three to eight subheadings throughout.

Principle 4: Use the "Inverted Pyramid Method"

When your readers are seriously considering a purchase, they will scroll all around your sales page. But the top of your page should still be used for the most pivotal information. To help visualize the placement of content, copywriters often invoke an old metaphor called the "Inverted Pyramid Method."

The concept is simple. Picture an inverted pyramid, and divide it into 4 horizontal slices. The top (and largest) slice is for your most important information. The second slice is for slightly less-important info. Then comes the third. And finally, the last and smallest slice is for your least important information.

Think of the top of the pyramid as holding your large and important page heading, followed by your most important paragraph—of descriptive text about your product. The hierarchy of importance reduces, as you progress down the page. Or to put it simply, you want to write your most important content up top, and your least important content at the bottom—gradually reducing in complexity as you progress down the page.

Principle 5: Mix-up your fonts and colors

In copywriting, nothing screams "don't read me" louder than a large wall of text. So don't do this to your reader. Instead, breakup your content—using multiple sizes of fonts and colors.

For web pitch pages, a large, bold font (like "Impact" or "Arial Bold") is often used for headlines, and may be colored red or blue. Similarly, bold fonts can be used for subheadings. And, for your ad copy, use a simple sanserif font—like Arial or Verdana.

There is significant debate about whether serif or sanserif fonts are easier to read. For the uninitiated, serif fonts have little arcs and curves at the edges of the letters (e.g. like the font Times New Roman), while sanserif fonts don't have any flourish (e.g. like Arial and Helvetica).

The most effective type of font might be dependent upon the niche you're in. But if you're in doubt, choose Arial for now, and keep it simple. Remember, what's most important is that your copy is easy to digest, and that your readers are familiar and comfortable reading your selected fonts.

The Second Draft Checklist

Remember, long-form pitch pages are (indeed) long. They're often not finished in one day. So don't feel you must rush the process. After you're done with your first draft, walk away from it for the night. And approach your pitch page again in the morning. Try to read it from top to bottom, and try to put yourself in the headspace of a person who has just discovered your website.

Yes, you will be fixing grammatical errors, misspellings, and typos. But your main goal today, is to tighten the copy.

- Look for the places in the copy where you have used too many words.
- Find the places where your message is not clear.
- Look for areas in your copy that need tweaking.
- Is your headline benefit-oriented?
- Does your message come across with ease?
- Do you empathize with the reader's problem?
- Have you convinced the reader that you have the best solution?
- Are you using bullet points effectively, to summarize your solution?
- Do you offer a money-back guarantee?
- Did you write a strong and compelling Call-to-Action?
- Did you incorporate urgency and scarcity into your copy?
- Do you have credible testimonials?

- Have you offered something extra, like a freebie or bonus?

Refer to your list of product features and benefits—to make sure you're touting the best your product can provide. You don't want to leave out something important—that might have converted a reader into a customer.

Ch. 11: SEO for Copywriters

In the previous chapter, we talked about copywriting for website pitch pages. Persuading your human readers to become paying customers is the primary goal of such content. However, there is another goal. Not only do we have to please the humans, but we have to please the robots as well. Namely, we have to please the Search Engines robots.

Every second of every day, thousands of little programs called "crawlers" are canvassing the internet, and recording every word they come across. These crawlers reside on servers—owned by the Search Engines of the world (like Google and Bing).

When the crawlers encounter a website, they download every word on the page, and place it into a database. Then, other programs process this information, and try to determine what this webpage is about. For humans, this is often an easy job. Humans have the ability to look at a webpage and (usually) they can (rather quickly) comprehend the intent and purpose of the webpage.

For machines, however, this chore is quite difficult. And that's why Google spends a lot of money—to hire some of the smartest computer scientists on the planet, to develop clever ways to examine this data, and determine what information it contains.

The exact algorithm by which this process works is a trade secret. (And Google changes it every month anyway.) But what we do know is that it all starts with keywords.

The birth of a new industry

When you type words into a Search Engine (like Google), say "red camera bags" this phrase is called your "search query." The query is received by a Google server. And then, the server examines millions of documents that feature the words "red camera bags." Then the server must make a decision—about which 10 websites (out of millions) to display to you at Google.com. This webpage of 10 search results is called the Search Engine Results Page (or "SERP" for short).

Google's job is to find the best ten links about "red camera bags" in the world, and display them to you, so you can decide which one to click on.

That's it.

Now, what if you own a company that sells red camera bags, but your web designer failed to type the words "red camera bag" anywhere on your website. Then, how is Google going to know that you sell "red camera bags?"

Well, they won't know…

And Google's users may never be able to find your webpage, nor will they ever know that you're in the camera bag business.

That's not good.

So, how can we ensure that people who search for "red camera bags" via Google, have a chance of discovering your business?

Perhaps we should have told our web content writer to make sure that the words "red camera bags" exist—somewhere on our website… Right?

Right.

It was this insight that inspired the birth of a new type of industry. An industry that now features thousands of startups, software tools, web apps, and marketing agencies—all promising to help your company (quote) "Get to the Top of Google!"

The name of this industry is "SEO."

What is "SEO"?

SEO stands for "Search Engine Optimization." And, (as the name implies) SEO is about optimizing your website content—so that your target customers will be able to find you via search engines (like Google).

The trick lies in identifying the words (called "keywords") that your target demographic is typing into Google. And then, sprinkling these keywords throughout your web content. (This is called "optimizing the content for search engines"—hence the term: "Search Engine Optimization")

Simple right?

It actually is, once you get the hang of how to do it...

How to do SEO.

We can break the SEO chore down into just two tasks:

- **Step 1**: Find the keywords that your target demographic is using—when they're searching for your product or service on Google.
- **Step 2**: Sprinkle these keywords into your web content.

Step 1: Find Keywords

Let's tackle step 1 now.

Our only goal is to create a long list of keyword phrases—that best describe your product or service?

Fortunately, Google provides us with a free tool that does just that. It's called the Google Keyword Planner. And it has been churning out billions of keyword phrases for over a decade.

The original intent of the Google Keyword Planner was to allow Google's advertisers to see which keywords their potential customers were typing into Google. But, soon after its release, website owners soon realized that this data could be used for SEO as well.

Google requests that you enter a credit card when you create a new account over at the Keyword Planner homepage. But don't fret, because (if you don't buy ads), then you don't have to actually pay for anything, once you log in. We're just interested in the keyword data, and this is free.

Downloading a list of keywords is easy. Once you're logged into the Google Keyword Planner interface, then type a few words into the memo box. This initial set of words you type, is called your "seed keywords." Because, it is from these "seeds" that Google will "sprout forth" additional keyword ideas. Typically you'll type in three or four seed keywords, and Google will return a list of about a thousand keyword ideas.

Once you've saved this list on your hard drive, it's time to pick out the ones that are most reflective of your product or service. Recall, in our example company, we sold "camera bags." So, typing the seed keyword "camera bags" into the Google Keyword Planner reveals many keywords like:

- camera case
- leather camera bag
- camera backpack
- camera bags for women
- nikon camera bag
- camera purse
- waterproof camera bag
- etc.

These are the keywords that the consumers (in your niche) are actually typing into Google. So now, our job is to determine which keywords (in this list), apply to our product.

- Is your camera bag made of leather?
- Can your camera bag be worn on the back? If so, then does it qualify as a "camera backpack."
- Is your camera bag specifically designed for women, or for a certain type of Nikon camera?

Remember, your goal is to identify which keywords apply to your product. Every product is different. So, ultimately, *only you* will know which keywords are more applicable. So, go through your own keyword list, and place a check next to every word that applies to your business.

Step 2: Sprinkle Keywords into your Content

In Step 2, it's time to sprinkle our selected keywords, into our webpage. You'll notice that a typical product webpage contains many of the same elements as any other business document.

1. The product name and headline rests along the top.
2. A subheading often follows that.
3. An attractive product image comes next.
4. Ad copy (and product information) sits throughout the page.
5. And a Call-to-Action rests at the bottom. (Usually in the form of a "Buy Button" or Phone Number.)

The trick in SEO (Search Engine Optimization) lies in our ability to massage our keywords (the ones we placed a checkmark next to), into the textual content of these five locations.

Why do we do this again?

Recall that Google's job is to keep a record of every webpage on the planet. And try to determine what these webpages are about. If a Google user is searching for "red camera bags" and your camera bag company neglected to place these words in your website content somewhere, then Google will never know you're selling "camera bags" at all.

Recall the list we generated in Step 1, contained words like:

- leather camera bag
- camera bags for women
- waterproof camera bag

So, suppose the "camera bag" product you're selling had these three features.

- Suppose the exterior was made of leather.
- Suppose that it was aimed at the female market.
- Suppose that the interior storage area was waterproof.

This means, that you have a product that (the people typing these words into Google), are probably looking for.

So, it's your job (as an SEO guy), to make sure the words like:

- "leather"
- "for women"
- "waterproof"

get into your website content, somewhere. (Along with the words "camera" and "bag" of course.)

When the keywords (that your demographic uses to refer to your product) have been tactfully inserted into your product webpage, then you have successfully "optimized" your webpage for the Search Engines.

Do you see why this industry is called "Search Engine Optimization?" Because that describes exactly what we're doing.

What are Long Tail Keywords?

As you gather keywords for your website, you'll notice that they come in varying sizes.

- Some keywords are short—like the keyword "camera."
- But some keywords are long—like the phrase "best cameras for outdoor photography."

The latter keyword contains five words in the keyword phrase. Keywords like this are sometimes referred to as "Long Tail Keywords."

Long Tail Keywords are usually longer in length (consisting of more words in the phrase). And, because there is so much specificity contained in the phrase, their search volume is much less. E.g. many more people in the world type the word "camera" into Google, than type the phrase "best cameras for outdoor photography" into Google.

So, because of this fact, some website owners avoid these more obscure phrases. But not so fast! Enlightenment is achieved here when you realize this:

Long Tail Keywords account for 70% of all web searches.

When taken individually, each Long Tail Keyword doesn't bring much traffic. But when you can sprinkle three, four, or five additional Long Tail Keywords on your webpage, then the traffic starts to add up.

Most importantly, almost by their very nature, Long Tail Keywords are not very competitive. In other words, millions of websites are competing for the word "camera." But far fewer webpages (on the internet) contain information about the keyword phrase "best cameras for outdoor photography."

So ideally, you'll be able to locate a large set of Long Tail Keywords for your niche, and massage these into your web copy. When you do, you'll be attracting people who are curious about your product, but also people with ancillary interests as well. Or, to put it another way, Long Tail Keywords help you cast a wider net, with which to lure search engine traffic.

Avoid keyword-stuffing:

Now, it's important to not go overboard with keywords. People who are new to the world of SEO, tend to think that "the more the merrier" rule applies. They think that they should sprinkle keyword phrases into every sentence of their copy, and that this will, in some way, lure more search engine traffic.

But this is not the case. After a keyword phrase appears in your content one or two times, then adding it again and again will not improve your results. The act of filling your text with keywords is called "keyword-stuffing." And it should be avoided. In fact, if you put too many keywords into your content, then there may even be a Google penalty for doing so—and they may send you *less traffic.*

Remember, it is the quality of your work that will help to lure more visitors to your website. So don't compromise your persuasive copy, for the sake of inserting keywords. Just make your text flow naturally, and insert keywords when appropriate, and, in such a way that they blend into the content and add value to copy. Your first focus should be to write compelling, and easy-to-read sales copy.

After you go through this process one time, the SEO chore is not difficult. And, adding this final bit of effort to a webpage, can be the difference between luring thousands of hungry Google users, and failing to lure any Google traffic at all.

So take this step seriously. SEO is a valuable addition to your "copywriting bag of tricks."

Ch. 12: Copywriting for Web Ads

When you use a search engine (like Google or Bing), or when you're browsing a news website, you'll notice the plethora of web ads—that run along the website's side or whizz across your field of view. Typically, these are PPC (or Pay-per-Click) ads. Whenever you get enticed into clicking one of these ads, the marketer pays the website owner (or media company) for your click. So, obviously, clicks are valuable.

More clicks, means more eyeballs looking at your product or service. And more eyeballs means more opportunities—to convert visitors into paying customers.

So how do you use your newfound copywriting skills, to write the most appealing web ad possible?

In the rules below, we'll show you how.

Rule 1: Tell an Interesting Story

Stories are a great way to capture anyone's attention—especially those potential clients, who were once in your position. People love a peek into the lives of other people. They want to know what makes you happy, angry, or excited. They want to know your deepest struggles, and how you overcame complex challenges in your life.

Now, PPC adverts typically don't feature much space. So there isn't room to write your entire memoir. However, you can use this space to tease your audience—and hint at a story you'll share with them, after they click your ad.

A typical teaser you've probably notice on web ads starts like this:

"How this stay-at-home mom earns $10,000 per month online!"

Does this ad sound familiar?

This ad is so ubiquitous because it works.

When this ad is read by women (who are also stay-at-home moms), then the congruous language causes them to naturally assume that the ad might apply to them. When a stay-at-home mother comes across this ad, she will wonder how the money was made, and desire to hear the complete story.

So, keep your ads personal. Use a story to talk about how someone suffered from the same problem that your target prospects have. (e.g., business issues, weight loss, money problems, family problems, etc.) Then, offer the solution that fixed this issue.

How to be a Good Boss and a Leader

Rule 2: State the Benefits

Why do we click on ads?

Ultimately, humans click on ads because they think the destination might benefit them, in some way. Preferably, in some immediate way.

Because of our preference for instantaneous fixes, you may want to avoid ad language like this:

- Download this 850-page eBook about growing organic vegetables.
- Try this quick course on the Mathematics of Machine Learning.
- Try our 37 Step plan to save $10 per month on your car insurance.

These ads list technically challenging details, rather than potential benefits. But, your focus should be on the benefits—i.e. the improvements that your product can bring to the life of your prospect. Listing technical features can be important. But they should not be used to hook in prospects in ad copy.

Rule 3: Use Emotionally Charged Words

Copywriting is a game of words. Changing one word can change the whole meaning of your message. In the same way, one emotional word in your ad, might connect with the emotions of your prospects.

Use *power words* to jog the memory of your target. Power words are intuitive words that immediately grab his or her attention— and trigger memories, emotions, or past experiences in their lives.

For example, when someone sees the word *embarrassed* in an ad, they will remember the time when they felt embarrassment, and this will make them curious to know more about what happened to the person in the copy—that made them feel this way.

Keep in mind that every market has its own set of power words. For example, the words *devastated* and *embarrassed* probably won't work if you're writing an ad for tomato sauce. (They'd be best for acne products.) But the words *scrumptious* and *mouthwatering* might be perfect for tomato sauce.

Rule 4: Use a "How to" Phrase

One of the most classic of formulas (for a PPC headline) is to start the hook off with a "how-to" sentence.

For example:

- How to secure $10,000 in seed funding for your startup.
- How to lose 10 pounds in 2 weeks.
- How to reduce wrinkles with this home remedy.

If you're trying to come up with an ad, and you're getting writer's block, then start by jotting down a few "how to" questions—that your product is able to solve.

Rule 5: Use Numbers

We've talked about the power of numbers in ad copy before. But when you're writing headlines for web ads, they're even more important. Your reader's eyes are naturally drawn to numbers in PPC ads. Ad text that features simple numbers get higher click-through-rates than ads without them.

That's why you'll often see ads like this:

- 3 step plan for quitting smoking.
- 5 effective tricks to keep weight off during the holidays.
- 10 workout exercises to get you "beach-body ready" this season.

Rule 6: Use Special Characters

Just as using numbers in your ad copy, tends to make it stick out, using special symbols (oddly) does too. Special keyboard characters—like the pound, ampersand, percentage, copyright, trademark, and asterisk symbols, tend to catch your audience's eye online.

Rule 7: Use Social Proof

Just because the PPC ad copy area is so small, doesn't mean you can waive the power of "social proof." Using social proof can be the most potent strategy for ad copy. As with all other copywriting hooks, when your online ad reader considers clicking on an ad, he naturally would like to know if your product has worked for others in the past.

So, in your ad copy, consider peppering in phrases like this:

- "As seen on TV."
- "used in over 50 countries!"
- "5-Star rated"

Rule 8: Don't forget the negative space

If you're writing text-only PPC ads, then it's often best to use every character allotted to you—so that your ad takes up the highest amount of real estate on your screen.

However, if your ad is a larger web ad—(perhaps a large rectangular shaped ad with a photo), then don't be afraid to use negative space. Recall that when negative space (or "white space") is positioned around your ad copy, it tends to "draw in the eye"—to focus upon the solitary text within the negative space. Thus, negative space can actually make your ad more appealing. Ads that are crammed with too many words in a tight space, tend to be difficult to read, and hence, are easy to ignore.

Rule 9: Don't skip the Call-to-Action

Sometimes, it's not easy for internet users to infer the next action step you'd like them to take. If you use the web a lot, it might be obvious to you—that a marketer is trying to get you to click on his blue link. But remember, people online have varying technical skill-levels. So, for some ads, it's best to simply tell them what to do—in the clickable ad headline itself.

 e.g. "Click here now to learn how to save $200 dollars on car insurance."

Just because your ad copy is brief doesn't always mean you should skip the Call-to-Action, and explicitly tell the user what you want him to do.

Ch. 13: Copywriting for Print & Direct Mail

Nobody reads newspapers anymore. At least that's what we hear… While it is true that the legacy media is dying out, it's important to be familiar with the copywriting process they utilize. Remember, the art of copywriting itself primarily evolved out of old-school print advertising. So there is value in understanding how it works.

Moreover, while social media, websites, and search engines have become a common part of marketing campaigns, traditional marketing (via print ads), still works. The business world hasn't completely shunned print advertising yet. Far from it. Many big-name successful web campaigns still use print advertisements to get most of their attention. Sometimes, you'll receive a print ad (in the form of a coupon or newspaper advert) that you can redeem at your favorite e-commerce website. Today, all roads lead to the web. But print advertisements are still often a point of first contact.

We'll discuss the various types of print advertisement briefly here.

Types of Print

Newspapers

If your business goal is to capture the attention of local consumers, then print ads are still an effective way to reach your audience. You can connect with your target prospects through the local paper, or run ads in national papers as well.

Magazines

With their high-color glossy pages, publishing your ad in a magazine is still a great way to market your brand. You can use magazine advertisements either to build a public image of your business, or to attract customers.

Directories

Before the days of Google, companies used to scrutinize over their ad copy in print directories—especially the Yellow Pages phone book.

The phone book isn't as popular as it once was, of course. But industry-specific trade publications and directories still have clout. Becoming a part of such directories provides more exposure to new potential clients, and gives your business an air of legitimacy.

Other Types of Print

Other common types of print-advertising includes:

- Newsletters

- Banners
- Billboards
- Flyers
- and Brochures

But of all the print adverts discussed thus far, Direct Mail is often the most profitable.

Direct Mail

It's the 21st century. And yet, you still arrive home from work (each day), to find your mailbox has become a junk mail cornucopia—of coupons, credit card applications, circulars, DVDs, and brochures.

Why is this?

Because this is called Direct Mail Advertising (or "Junk Mail"). It accounts for over 40% of all US Mail sent. And is (often) the most profitable form of advertising—even to this day.

Yep. Believe it or not, direct mail still works.

There are still a lot of coupon clippers out there. And there is a certain segment of the population who is more likely to respond to a letter than an email. While over 45% of us immediately throw out our junk mail (without even reading it), of the people who do interact with it, around 60% will visit a website—after being influenced by a direct mail offer.

We mention this here to encourage our younger readers to give Direct Mail a chance, as part of your marketing efforts. All of the same copywriting tricks still apply. But below, we've listed a few print-specific tips.

Copywriting Tips for Direct Mail and Print

Tip 1: Your audience might be older

Young people don't respond to paper coupons and fliers like their parents once did. Nor do they buy newspapers. So before you sit down to write your copy, understand that the demographic that reads print ads, will almost always be an older crowd.

Tip 2: Use Headings and Subheadings

As in other marketing domains, the printed headline will be the first piece of copy that your customer reads. But unlike other marketing media (like PPC ads), print headlines often include a subheading too. (Sometimes several.) Remember, the top heading is "the hook." And subheadings should act to further lure the reader in—deeper down into your web copy.

- If the headline is a question, then your sub-headline can be the answer.
- If the headline is a cryptic statement, then your sub-headline can reveal more about the topic.

Tip 3: Stay on message

Just as people easily get confused when looking at complicated text bodies online, they also get confused if you hit them with too many print options or messages.

So don't promote every product in your catalog with your print ad. Instead, choose one product or service to feature in your ad. Then, craft your ad copy and design around this message.

Tip 4: Combine Images and Copy

With print ads, words are often not sufficient on their own. Print ad copy works best when paired with imagery of course. Ads with images have been shown to increase conversions. So, unlike with text ads or even PPC ads, print ads tend to be more photo-heavy. That is to say, the image itself may act as the primary lure. A page in a glossy magazine that only features text, may not win you many customers.

So add visuals to "paint the picture" of your product or service. Your photos are not just for decorative purposes. Rather, they must go hand-in-hand, with the message you're trying to deliver via your ad copy.

When selecting photos, try this criteria:

1. Use pictures that evoke a powerful emotional response, like babies, animals (kittens and puppies), food, sports, etc.
2. Avoid using black-and-white images, or dull images. Color photos usually do better.

3. Select images that are relevant and harmonious with your copy. And that resonates with your target demographic.

Selecting the right photo can really give your ad a boost. But don't allow your stunning imagery to cause you to abandon the copywriting principles we've discussed earlier. Magazines are full of ads with amazing visuals, but without any action step for the reader to take next, the ad might flop anyway.

Typically, unless you're doing large scale branding, your ads should make a single point about your product or service. And explicitly tell the reader what solution it is offering, and why they should choose it.

Tip 5: Keep your Call-to-Action Simple

The Call-to-Action for print ads may be a bit different—than for other types of marketing. Typical print ad Calls-to-Action involve making a phone call, typing in a URL, or (more commonly these days) scanning a QR Code with your smart phone.

What's most important for print ads, is that you (again), remember that your customers have varying levels of technical skill. Older people often have no idea how to use QR Codes, while younger people don't like placing phone calls.

Most of your potential customers can comprehend a web URL. But if your URL is difficult to spell or remember, then, translating this information from the printed page, to a web browser can be tedious. Additionally, directing your users to subfolders on your website adds an even trickier layer of complexity. So, be sure your

URLs are "easy to type" If your URL on the printed page looks like this:

http://www.StevensAirConditioningRepair.com/coupon/ 333214579

then, you're doing it wrong.

Notice how Apple directs users from their print ads, to their iPod webpage. They simply write:

Apple.com/ipod

That's it.

Nice and simple, right?

Remember, nobody likes to type a bunch of slashes, numbers, colons, and three "w's." So, if you include a URL in your Call-to-Action, just be sure to keep it simple.

Ch. 14: Copywriting for Press Releases

Press Releases are becoming a bit dated these days. But, (especially for larger companies) they can be an effective marketing tool—to bring media attention for your newly formed business or product.

They can be published on your company website, in trade magazines, newsletters, etc. So, a press release can help your business establish a strong reputation in its industry. However, crafting an effective press release (that will actually get picked up and read) is the hard part.

The best press releases feature some sort of compelling story or novel introduction. Start out by structuring your press release like this:

- First, write a great title. For press releases, the title functions in much the same way as the ad headline— that we've discussed before. It's designed to lure in your prospective reader. So, don't use something dull or bland, such as "So and so company signed a deal today..." Instead, your title should immediately hook the reader, and make him want to read more.

- Next, write a compelling first paragraph which summarizes the relevant news. Provide information about the event using the five W's (who, what, where, when, why) and one H (how).

- Elaborate on the business and its key people in the second paragraph. Then, go on to mention some credible testimonials, or a decent quote. Insert references to other articles in the industry.

- And, consider linking your news to a wider event—to give it a future spin.

We've listed four important tips for Press Releases below.

Don't focus on "you"

When you're writing a press release, put yourself in the shoes of a journalist. He will skim through the press release to find out if the story will benefit his readers at all.

If the answer is "yes," then he won't have any trouble promoting it. If the answer is "no," then ask yourself why it didn't appeal to his target audience. Ideally, your press release should present an appealing story about your company or products, that is relevant to your prospective clientele.

Make sure it's topical

Press Releases are most effective when they coincide with other topical events. So if you can blend the release of a new product, with some sort of recent news even, then this makes your press release newsworthy, and prone to conversation.

A press release is not a sales pitch

A press release is a tool to deliver novel information. But it's usually not written in a sales-pitchy fashion. Nor, is its purpose necessarily to coax the reader to purchase anything. So, the content of your press release should be free of elaborate adjectives, and written in a factual manner. Keep it short and sweet, and your readers will appreciate that.

Ch. 15: Copywriting as a Career

We can hardly write an "intro to copywriting" book, without including a chapter on pursuing copywriting as a career. We hope, at this point in the book, you're inspired to apply these techniques in your own marketing efforts, as well as inspired enough to do copywriting full time perhaps.

If you love to write, and feel that you're good at tailoring words into stunning, persuasive sentences, then copywriting might be the profession for you.

The good news is, you don't need a college degree (or any formal training at all) to start a career in copywriting. But being familiar with the different types of industries that employ copywriters is helpful. We've listed several here.

Industries for Copywriters

1. Advertising Agencies

Most copywriters work in advertising, in one form or another. Fans of the television show "Mad Men" got a glimpse of what a 1960s New York City advertising agency might have looked like. The reality is a bit less saucy perhaps. But the show reveals some of what copywriters do each day. Working on print ads for products or services, creating corporate slogans, scripts for television and radio advertisements, infomercials, and broadcasts. Many companies (big and small) pay Advertising Agencies to produce their marketing creatives.

Working for a large advertising agency (like Omnicom, TBWA Worldwide, or Dentsu) has its benefits—because the work is more stable than freelancing of course. To get an agency copywriter job, experience helps, and the high-paying jobs are not for newbies. Still, you can stand out from the competition, if you have a background in emerging fields—like digital marketing and social media.

2. In-House Corporate Copywriters

Larger companies often employ in-house writers of various types (including copywriters). They are typically responsible for producing copy for advertising campaigns, or even for employee manuals, or technical documents. They may write company reports, product descriptions, case studies, make branding decisions, write proposals, promotional messages, taglines, and even web content.

3. Freelance Internet Marketers

Every aspect of Internet Marketing relies on copywriting. Copy is pivotal in Search Engine Optimization, Pay-per-Click Advertising, website landing page design, and (especially), in email marketing. So whether you're writing copy for your own website, or taking on contract work, there is plenty of work to be found in internet marketing.

If you want to go freelance, you have the benefit of being able to set your own schedule. This is why so many freelance content creators, consider their jobs to be "lifestyle careers." Because this sort of work allows them to "live off their laptop" and travel while you work.

Income while working as a freelance copywriter, often comes on a project-per-project basis. So, when you're first starting out, your salary might fluctuate unpredictably. But, freelancers who are able to foster connections, and develop a name for themselves, often make a very impressive salary.

How to Improve your Copywriting Skillset

Like so many other things in life, *copywriting* might take a weekend to learn, but a lifetime to master. It's an exercise in continuous improvement of course. But below, we've listed three tips to keep you moving in the right direction.

1. Read a lot

Read copywriting handbooks, websites, copywriting blogs, classic print copywriting books, or any other copywriting literature you can get your hands on. But most importantly, get used to reading ads, and analyzing how you feel while you're reading them.

Try to identify the tricks that the copywriter used to get your attention. Don't read the ad the way normal, casual readers do. Instead, scan the ad slowly. Ask yourself about the word-selection in the ad. Why did the designer choose the color red, instead of the color green? How are the adjectives in the copy affecting your mood?

In fostering your copywriting skills, learning how to read (and perceive) the adverts of other copywriters, is often more important than simply reading books *about copywriting* itself.

2. Write a lot

American educator Edgar Dale (1900-1985) is famous for the oft-quoted dictum:

> "People generally remember 90% of what we teach."

While the original research behind this quote is spotty, and Edgar Dale himself told people "not to take the number too seriously" the intent of the expression is still sound. If you want to get better at something, then doing it, writing about it, and teaching it, is probably one of the fastest ways to improve.

You get better at writing when you write.

So, if you're really considering copywriting as a career then, start writing ads and writing about copywriting, as soon as possible. You don't have to actually have a copywriting job, to start writing copy. Just find a product that you're a fan of, and look at their current body of ad copy. Then, see how you could improve it yourself.

Consider starting a blog, and record your newfound advertising epiphanies. Place bits of copy on your blog, and see how your friends and family respond to your creations.

If you're really serious about copywriting, then put your money where your mouth is. And buy some Google Ads for an affiliate product.

Or, if all this is too scary at first, then just write about whatever you're passionate about. In the early days of your career, your primary goal should be to:

"Keep that keyboard clicking!"

That's it.

If you can keep your fingers on the keyboard, and start generating content (of any kind), then this is better than taking no action at all.

Don't be worried if your initial set of words are mere dribble. You don't have to actually show anyone your content if you don't want to. What's important is that your brain will be learning as you are typing. And each day, when you approach the keyboard again, the words will flow, just a little bit easier. If you've ever sat behind an older newspaper reporter before, then you might know what I mean. Some reporters can sit down at a keyboard, and blast out news-worthy content, without even glancing at their laptop. Just as in every other human pursuit, writing is a skill that we gradually master. Until, someday, the skill is so effortless, that we wonder why other people find it difficult to do.

3. Keep a Portfolio

When you're done writing, save your work. Perhaps you'll want to print it out, or save it in a journal, or back it up to the cloud. But save your work somewhere.

Having a historical body of your own words is important, for several reasons. First, each word you type is a trophy, that we show to the world. It's a symbol that a conscious mind was here, and that you had something to say.

But, most importantly, keeping a long trail of words allows your future self to look back, and see all the work you've written. And understand how you've improved over time. This is pivotal. Because it's typically not healthy to compare yourself to others. But it can be quite fruitful to compare yourself to the person you were yesterday. If you can save your words, look through them, and see gradual improvement over time, this will encourage you to keep going—to improve even more, each day.

Applying to Jobs

If you're pursuing one of the more prized marketing positions in the corporate sector, then becoming intimately familiar with a specific niche is often key. The copy you'd write for the beauty industry, is not the same copy you'd write to sell Harley Davidson

Motorcycles. In the crazy world of advertising, the best copywriters tend to specialize.

Know your niche market, inside and out. Learn what the competition is up to. Perhaps, try to master an industry-specific marketing strategy—that you can showcase to leaders in the niche.

If you're just starting out, it's often best to pick a particular product or service that you're a fan of. And then, start working in your niche for small companies at first, with the intent of moving up to larger clients later.

Be a man of many hats

Another way to increase your own salability, is to master ancillary marketing skills. Remember, marketing is a vast domain. And, a company that is looking to hire a copywriter, is often in the market for multiple employees—who wear many different hats. So, you provide a lot of value to your employer by being skilled at more than one thing.

As we've already discussed, learning internet marketing (in all its forms) is a major asset. If you can do copywriting, as well as SEO, and if you have a working knowledge of webpage design, then you are in a particularly enviable positon indeed. And, you'll be able to market your many skills to almost any company that interviews you.

Going to Interviews

When you receive a call back to go to a copywriting interview, then this is your chance to nail the job and shine. But, perhaps you don't know what to say, nor what you should ask from the interviewer?

Meetings like this go well when your existing body of marketing content is congruous with the type of content produced by the company. For example, if you're interviewing for a car company, and you've been doing marketing in the auto industry for 30 years, then you're an obviously viable candidate.

But, even if you have no direct experience in the industry, that doesn't mean you can't show up to the interview prepared. Before going, research the company thoroughly online. Specifically, take note of the marketing campaigns they've launched through the years. If you see that they had a successful minivan ad five years ago, then look in your existing body of work, and see if you have any marketing material that is in any way congruous.

If not, then just make up your own ad. And be honest about it. Bring your own re-created minivan ad to the interview, and explain how you would have approached the assignment.

Common Interview Questions for Copywriting Jobs

Let's go over three common interview questions, that are likely to come up when you're applying to copywriting jobs.

Question 1: "What assignment have you completed recently, that is most similar to our marketing campaigns?"

As mentioned before, advertising companies tend to specialize in one niche or another. So they're most comfortable hiring people who have already created campaigns in their niche. If you have never worked in their niche, then try to come up with some mockups before the interview, detailing how you would have handled the account.

Question 2: "Which campaign was the most challenging for you?"

Campaigns can be tough. So here, the interviewer wants to know which parts of the job you find challenging. Decide on a past project, and speak about it honestly. This shows that you are not afraid of challenging work and you won't break down under pressure. Remember, people often value honesty more than most other human traits.

Question 3: What topics are you most comfortable writing about?

No copywriter can write about every topic with ease. People's interests vary wildly. Generally, it's easier to write about topics you enjoy, and it makes the daily-grind more gratifying. For example, a copywriter who hates the fashion industry, can still begrudgingly get through the workday—and produce fashion industry copy. But if he hates the niche, then scribing each and every sentence might feel torturous.

So, don't put yourself through that! If you're more of a fan of "canoes and camping gear," then you probably shouldn't be applying for a marketing job at "Versace of New York."

Keep "Pounding the Pavement"

Going to interviews at some of the bigger advertising firms can be competitive and stressful. Moreover, you may be competing against applicants with decades of marketing experience. So don't get discouraged if the best positions don't fall in your lap during your first week of pounding the pavement.

Prepare yourself (emotionally) for failures. If an interview doesn't go particularly well, then, learn from it, and resume your hunt. Also, consider asking for feedback from the hiring manager himself. Typically, they'll gladly point to some part of your repertoire that is currently lacking. And if you were to focus on this skill before the next interview, then your chance of getting the next job is likely greater.

Ch. 16: Hiring a Copywriter

When you're a small business owner, you have to do everything. Every job is your job.

Consequently, many small business owners start off doing their own copywriting. This trend often persists, even after the company is quite large. Even the late great Steve Jobs was known for participating in the copywriting of marketing campaigns, well after Apple was an established multinational conglomerate.

So, if you're running a dynamic business, that keeps growing, then you'll eventually have to hire a copywriter or marketing company. Hopefully, after reading this book, you are well aware of the type of skills one needs to be successful at copywriting. But, in this chapter, we'll try to teach you a few ways to spot these skill in others.

Below, we've listed all the steps we take, when hiring a copywriter.

Steps to Hire a Copywriter

Step 1. Where do you find Copywriters?

The location in which you hunt for your new copywriter is dependent on the type of job you're offering. If you're merely looking for a temporary writer (to work on a project-by-project basis), then many websites facilitate this hunt. Upwork and Fiverr might be your first two choices.

If you're looking for a full-time employee, who will show up at your office from 9-5 each day, then you'd typically look on Craigslist or LinkedIn.

Step 2. What do you want from your copywriter?

Before writing your job description, be sure that you are crystal clear on the various types of writer jobs available. We spent a lot of time (at the start of this book) distinguishing between the various types of writing jobs.

Remember a Copywriter is not necessarily a Copyeditor, which is not necessarily a Content Writer. (Copywriter, Copyeditor, Content Writer… these are three different positions—requiring three different skillsets.) But, even people who work in the industry, often confuse these terms. So make sure you're hiring the right person!

Here are some reasons you might need a copywriter for your business:

- Your ad copy is not bringing in enough customers.
- Your copy is too complicated and dry, or too technically focused.

- You need a new pair of experienced eyes, to examine your marketing efforts, and advise possible changes.

- You're launching a new product, and you need extra help—to broaden your marketing horizons.

- You run a business, but don't have the time, nor the patience for copywriting. So you need someone to help you out.

Any of these reasons might be enough to start your hunt for a copywriter. But remember, that not all copywriters are marketers or internet marketers. They may be able to write ad copy, but they might not know the first thing about pay-per-click advertising or how to build website landing pages. Copywriters are not "SEO guys."

Marketing (in general) is a large, complex, and dynamic field. So be warned against dumping the labor of an entire marketing agency, onto the shoulders of just one person.

Step 3. Estimate costs

If you're hiring copywriters on a project-by-project basis, they're usually paid by the hour, and fees are highly variable. While some copywriters on Fiverr will write you something for $5 dollars, you'll typically be looking for a deliverable with more experience behind it. Most decent U.S. copywriters will charge a minimum of $35 dollars per hour. But the most experienced and famous copywriters have been known to charge thousands per hour!

Step 4. Ask for samples

To separate the wheat from the chaff, it helps to request work samples from your prospective copywriter. Ideally, they'll have an existing portfolio of work. And if they don't, then this is a red flag. In a best-case scenario, copywriters will keep "before and after" samples—showing how they were able to turn around a marketing campaign, and increase sales with their copy.

Step 5: Interviewer's Cheat Sheet

If you're considering hiring a copywriter as a full-time employee, then you might add these questions to your interview process:

1. How did you get into the copywriting profession?
2. What is your favorite company (or brand) that you take inspiration from?
3. Is there a product or service you prefer to write for?
4. What's the best marketing campaign, you've ever been a part of?

Working with a Copywriter

Once you've finally brought a copywriter onboard, the workflow often is easiest if you strive to familiarize them with your industry first. The more they understand your niche, the more likely their copy is to connect with your audience. So, provide them with some background, about your corporate history, products and services, competitors, and, your general sales and marketing strategy. Ideally, you'll keep this information readily available and updated, as part of your human resources efforts. Most importantly, your company should have a style guide.

Prepare a Company Style Guide

A company's "Style Guide" is like a blueprint for a copywriter. It ensures consistency throughout all your marketing material. Typically, a style guide might include the following elements:

#1 A Buyer Persona
A Buyer Persona is very useful for reminding your marketers who your target clientele is. Typically, buyer personas are just a one-page bio—depicting the characteristics, hopes, and pain-points, of your hypothetical "average customer."

Buyer Personas give your writer information about who his copy is targeting. Many writers will actually attach these characteristics to a doll or stuffed animal, and keep the toy in view, while they're writing copy.

#2 Voice and Tone guidelines
Provide examples for your copywriter—which defines the voice and tone of your prior marketing efforts. You should be keeping a list of adjectives that you (and your customers) have used to describe your product in the past.

For example, if you're selling paintball guns, do your clients merely "play games" with them? Or do your clients (quote) "wage realistic simulated warfare games" with them?

This is an important distinction. Because the text we choose here will affect our target clientele in different ways. Remember, in copywriting, we usually strive to refer to our products the same way our customers do.

#3 Maintain Layout and Formatting specifications

Every company has a unique way of formatting and presenting their text and marketing materials. Typically designers will keep a lookup table for colors and fonts, as well as more technical specifications—like paper weight, product photos, and logo formats.

Now, you don't have to create a company encyclopedia of pedantic technical details. But do strive to maintain a set of documents that reflect your company's unique format. In the least, companies will have a set of prior marketing campaign documents to pull from—featuring corporate letterhead, logos, and font specifications. This is usually enough to get your copywriter started. Corporate themes change over time. But customer conversions are highest when there is harmony between the design themes used in all your marketing material—from your paper envelopes, to your website landing pages.

Ch. 17: Conclusion

Similar to chess, copywriting takes a week to learn, but a lifetime to master. Remember, there is an **art and a science** to copywriting. Just as in all the writing professions, it's an exercise in continuous, daily improvement. But with each ad you write, you do indeed get a little bit better, every day.

As my 4th grade English teacher Mrs. Weinstein used to say:

"Your ability to write will be aided by
how much you read."

This is true.

Each time your mind considers a sentence (be it from the web, print, or conversation), this sentence becomes a part of the language centers of your own brain. So, the best way to improve your copywriting, is to improve your "copy reading." Keep reading books, ads, webpages, fliers, and keep flipping through magazines. As the marketing material of the world scurries across your field of view, take time for introspection, and ask yourself:

- How is this ad making me feel right now?

- Why did this ad grab my attention?
- Why have I been buying the same tissue paper for 10 years, even though there are cheaper options?
- Do I really believe that cheaper shampoo makes my hair look worse?
- Why do I feel that Product A is safer than Product B?

Learning to recognize and understand your own buying-behavior, is the first step to being able to influence the buying-behavior in others.

Often, your most important copywriting training won't come from a book. Rather, it will be based on a long history of introspective experiences—in which you're constantly pinging your own brain, and asking yourself: "Why did I just click that?"

Answering this question is when the real learning happens! Good copywriters strive to be cognizant of their underlying machinations of their own subconscious—the ancient motivators, that drive human buying behavior. When you understand how these triggers are working within your own mind, then you'll be more apt to invoke these triggers in your target consumer.

When used in this manner, words can become a powerful tool of persuasion. The English author Edward Bulwer-Lytton was right, when (in 1839), he proclaimed:

"The pen is mightier than the sword."

Indeed it is.

And copywriters (who know how to coax large populations of people into action) are able to prove this adage every day.